THE DIMENSION
OF THE PRESENT MOMENT

CHINGIZ AITMATOV
TAMAS ACZEL
VACLAV HAVEL
MIROSLAV HOLUB
TADEUSZ KONWICKI
KRZYSZTOF KIESLOWSKI
MILAN KUNDERA
CZESLAW MILOSZ
JOSEF SKVORECKY
ALEXANDER SOLZHENITSYN
ALEKSANDER TISMA
ANDRZEJ WAJDA

faber and faber

The Dimension of the Present Moment by Miroslav Holub
is published by Faber and Faber in April 1990

NEW EUROPE!

30

Editor: Bill Buford
Commissioning Editor: Lucretia Stewart
Assistant Editor: Tim Adams
Managing Editor: Angus MacKinnon
Assistant to the Editor: Ursula Doyle

Managing Director: Caroline Michel
Publisher/Consultant: Alice Rose George
Financial Manager: Robert Linney
Subscriptions: Gillian Kemp, Carol Harris
Advertising and Circulation: Alison Ormerod
Office Assistant: Stephen Taylor

Russian Editorial Adviser: Jana Howlett
Picture Research: David Brownridge
Design: Chris Hyde
Executive Editor: Pete de Bolla
US Associate Publisher: Anne Kinard, Granta, 250 West 57th Street, Suite 1316, New York, NY 10107.

Editorial and Subscription Correspondence: Granta, 2–3 Hanover Yard, Noel Road, Islington, London N1 8BE. Telephone: (071) 704 9776. Fax: (071) 704 0474. Subscriptions: (071) 837 7765.
A one-year subscription (four issues) is £19.95 in Britain, £25.95 for the rest of Europe, and £31.95 for the rest of the world.
All manuscripts are welcome but must be accompanied by a stamped, self-addressed envelope or they cannot be returned.

Set by Cambridge Photosetting Services, Cambridge.

Granta is published by Granta Publications Ltd and distributed by Penguin Books Ltd, Harmondsworth, Middlesex, England; Viking Penguin, a division of Penguin Books USA Inc, 375 Hudson Street, New York, NY 10014, USA; Penguin Books Australia Ltd, Ringwood, Victoria, Australia; Penguin Books Canada Ltd, 2801 John Street, Markham, Ontario, Canada L3R 1BR; Penguin Books (NZ) Ltd, 182-190 Wairau Road, Auckland 10, New Zealand. This selection copyright © 1990 by Granta Publications Ltd.

The editors wish to thank Michael Glenny, Rose Marie Morse and Elisabeth Ruge.

The translations for this issue have been made possible, in part, by a grant from the Wheatland Foundation, New York.

Cover by Chris Hyde.

Granta 30, Spring 1990. Reprinted October, 1990.

ISBN 9780140142983

CLANDESTINE IN CHILE
by **Gabriel García Márquez**

In 1973, a portly, dark-haired, bearded film director fled Chile after the military coup.Twelve years later he returned, slim, fair, clean-shaven, bringing with him a false passport, a false name, a false past and a false wife.

What kind of man trades his own identity for an invented one? What compels an exile to return to the country where he is on the wanted list?

'This is García Márquez at his least baroque and most self-effacing; understanding that the story has no need of magical realist embellishment he tells it plainly in the form of Littin's first-person narrative. That is to say; he acts as Littin's ghost. Márquez once rashly swore never to publish a novel until Pinochet fell. His broken promise will no doubt have made this book feel all the sweeter.' Salman Rushdie, *Times Literary Supplement*

'Such is García Márquez's uncanny power of evocation that Littin's experiences become ours, and Pinochet's Chile materializes before our eyes. Littin's underground adventure, far from approaching a starring role for the director – portrayed as a notably incompetent, almost Clouseau-like clandestine – dramatizes the heroic resistance of countless other Chileans, some successful, many others tortured or disappeared over the past fifteen years.' *The Guardian*

On 28 November 1986, in Valparaiso, the Chilean authorities impounded and burned 15,000 copies of this book.

March publication paperback, £3.99.

ISBN: 0 140 14015 8

GRANTA BOOKS

CONTENTS

GRAHAM SWIFT
LOOKING FOR
JIŘÍ WOLF

A t the beginning of December 1988, I visited Czechoslovakia for the first time. I knew then about the case of Jiří Wolf, though it was not the prime reason for my visit. A month before, I had been in Stockholm, where my publisher, Thomas von Vegesack, is president of the International PEN Writers in Prison Committee. I told him that I had been invited to Czechoslovakia for the publication of a Slovak translation of one of my books, and he reminded me that Jiří Wolf was a prisoner 'adopted' by both the Swedish and English Committees. Perhaps I could ask some discreet questions.

I got some information on Wolf from the PEN Committee in London and did indeed ask questions during my visit. I discovered, rapidly enough, that the opportunity to ask questions was limited by the general constraints on talking freely. Also, for most of my visit I was in Bratislava, the Slovak capital, while Wolf was a Czech from Bohemia. I spent just a couple of days in Prague. The fact remains that when I did ask questions, I got the same response: genuine, not simulated, ignorance. No one seemed to have heard of him.

My visit made a strong impression on me, in part because I had read the dossier on Wolf, and some of Wolf's own words, just before my departure. Frankly, the country depressed me. I encountered a great deal of individual kindness, above all from my Slovak translator, Igor, a reservedly humorous man and a good friend, but I felt that I was in a land that had gone into internal emigration. It was cut off from its own best resources, and even the things that could be simply admired, like the beautiful buildings of Prague, seemed false and irrelevant.

Much of this may be the standard Western reaction. I felt a mixture of gladness and guilt on returning home, and for some while I was haunted by my impressions and in particular—though here I had only imagination to go on—by thoughts of Jiří Wolf. I wrote letters on his behalf. I heard from the British Embassy in Prague that his case had been raised during the Vienna meeting of the Conference on Security and Co-operation in Europe, though to no apparent avail. It was only to be hoped that he would at least survive the remainder of his prison sentence, which was due to end during 1989.

I did not know if and when I might return to Czechoslovakia. I certainly felt, from my limited knowledge and from what I had picked up on the spot, that despite Gorbachev the situation in the country was unlikely to improve. It might even worsen. A typical joke at the time of my first visit ran:

Karel: This perestroika is getting real bad.

Pavel: Yes, soon we Czechoslovaks will have to send tanks into Russia.

But we have all been surprised by the events of the last year. And, almost a year to the day after I had left it, I found myself returning to a Prague in the grip of what was variously called, depending on your translator, a 'smiling', a 'gentle' or a 'tender' revolution. My chief purpose, with some five days to achieve it, was to find Jiří Wolf.

Wolf's case may be as unexceptional as it is awful. His is a history of harassment, imprisonment and maltreatment which has been documented—largely self-documented—and which seized my interest. There are many other documented cases, and time has yet to reveal, if it ever will completely, the extent of undocumented cases. Prisons are often the last sections of society to be touched by political reform and though, as I write, Czechoslovakia has a new government, it would be a mistake to suppose that the country no longer has institutions and personnel accustomed to the regular abuse of human rights.

W olf was born in 1952. The facts I knew of his life were these. An orphan, he was brought up in state homes. He is of Jewish origin, with no living relatives save one half-sister. He married, has a son, but was divorced in 1978. He has worked in the uranium mines at Pribram, also as a driver and stoker. Apart from his writings in and about prison, he has written an autobiographical work, *Mrtvá cesta* ('Dead Journey') and a novel, *Čérné barety* ('Black Berets'). In 1977 he signed the Charter 77 declaration and in 1978 was arrested for possessing 'anti-State', 'anti-Party' and 'anti-Socialist' documents, and subsequently sentenced to three years' imprisonment for 'subversion of the Republic'. He was committed to Minkovice prison.

At his trial Wolf complained that he had been forced to admit guilt under physical and psychological pressure, and his sentence was extended by six months for 'false accusations'. He was transferred from Minkovice to Valdice, a prison of the harshest category and perhaps the most notorious prison in Czechoslovakia, and released in 1981. He remained active and was subject to harassment and arrest. In May 1983 he was charged with 'subversion in collusion with foreign agents' and 'divulging official secrets' for allegedly passing information to the Austrian Embassy about conditions in Minkovice. He was sentenced to six years' imprisonment and in 1984 found himself again in Valdice.

Wolf's prison writings, covering a ten year period of imprisonment, are grim and harrowing. His 'regime' was one of terror, cold, hunger, isolation and deprivation. Prisoners are allowed one visit, of one hour only, and one parcel every ten months, though these minimal rights are often denied. They are exploited as cheap labour. They are denied clothing sent to them. They are subject to indiscriminate beatings, some of which prove fatal, and to medical neglect. They are forced to eat food off the floor, food which is in any case inadequate, as prisoners are known to cut their wrists in order to drink their blood. Or just to cut their wrists. In 1988 Wolf was permitted a brief visit by two American doctors. They found him in poor shape but were not allowed to leave vitamins or medicines for ulcer treatment. Wolf told them he contemplated suicide.

I arrived in Prague with little more than a list of possibly useful names and telephone numbers. I had established from the PEN Committee in London that Wolf had indeed been released, in bad health, on 17 May 1989, but his whereabouts were unknown and information unforthcoming. I had recommendations and promises of help from various sources and, via a BBC unit in Prague, the name of a man, Miloš, who might act, if needed, as interpreter and co-searcher. I had phoned him from London, along with a number of other people in Prague. Miloš knew nothing of Wolf but, with only limited free time, was ready to help. Other responses, where there was not an immediate language problem, were co-operative, but no one, just as a year ago, seemed to have more than a dim notion of Wolf.

I had phoned Igor in Bratislava, who was prepared to meet me in Prague the following Saturday; also an editor in Prague, who again knew nothing of Wolf but promised to do what she could and in any case to arrange some meetings with other Czech writers. All these phone calls I prefaced with a wary 'Please tell me if I should not discuss certain matters on the phone.' This met with varying reactions, from 'Say what you like' to 'It's probably bugged but what the hell?' It was hard to tell if this was bravado or if a real barrier of caution had been lifted.

I arrived on Wednesday, 6 December. The 'gentle revolution', if it was to be dated from the ungentle night of 17 November, when police brutality had ignited the will of the people, was barely two weeks old. The opposition group Civic Forum was locked in intense negotiation with a government that still held a firm communist majority. The last big demonstration had been on Monday the fourth. A general strike was threatened for the following Monday.

It has to be said that on the streets the general impression was one of calm normality—if normality is not an ambiguous term for Czechoslovakia. The Czechoslovak flag was everywhere. Unostentatious red, white and blue tags adorned hats and lapels. In the central part of the city posters and information sheets, many of them hand-written and seemingly modest, were thick on walls and shop fronts. On *Staroměstské náměstí*, Old Town Square, a huge Christmas tree vied with a vigil of striking students beneath the statue of Jan Hus.

'Gentle revolution' seemed appropriate. But the gentleness was deceptive as well as touching. Optimism was being under-mined by a jitteriness at the extreme fragility of the situation. This was a week when things might go either way. The 'smiling' revolution might lose its smile or show its teeth. People admitted to violent swings of mood from euphoria to depression. Little things told a lot: a confusion in the use of the pronouns 'we' and 'they'; the tiredness in people's eyes; the hoarseness in their voices. They had been doing a lot of shouting, a lot of talking, aware of never before having been able to talk so much. But old habits die hard: a sudden glance over the shoulder or to the side would be followed by a self-reproachful but still worried laugh.

I made a round of phone calls, including one to Miloš, and arranged to meet the editor, Alžběta, that evening. She had done a great deal of homework since my call from London and had fixed meetings for me with the writers Ludvík Vaculík and Ivan Klima, with the possibility of meeting other writers and dissidents. She had found out nothing further about Wolf but she had made her own list of contacts to compare with mine. My priority was to find Wolf, but, viewing things pessimistically, I wanted to keep my options open. If there was no trail to follow, I didn't want my time to be empty.

I confess to more complex motives. What drew me to Wolf was, in part, that he was unknown (in more ways than one, it seemed). He was a writer, but he appeared to have no standing in contemporary Czechoslovak literature. Quite possibly, he was not an exceptionally good writer, although very brave, and his literary career had simply been eclipsed by his activist and prison experience.

A certain myth of the 'Czechoslovak Writer' seems to have arisen, at least in Western eyes: a figure automatically martyred and ennobled—banned, exiled—for the very act of writing. There may be both truth and justice in this sanctification: Václav Havel is a genuine intellectual hero who has won the spontaneous following of a people. But I suspected that the elevation of prominent writers into political symbols had obscured many 'unknowns'—writers and non-writers—and that it was perhaps unfair to the individuality of the prominent figures themselves. I wanted to test the myth, to discover whether writers resented or accepted their politicization and how they viewed a future which might restore their freedom but also remove some of their politically conferred cachet. To all this, Wolf's case would lend a rigorous perspective.

I met Alžběta at six. I gave her a copy I had of the PEN dossier on Wolf (unsure whether this was still a risky document to carry around), and we went to make inquiries at Civic Forum's new headquarters, a short distance from Alžběta's office. I anticipated the problem that, given the hectic pace of events, people who might otherwise be able to help would be too busy. I placed strong hopes on contacting members of the unofficial network VONS—the Committee for the Unjustly Prosecuted—which worked to monitor and publish details of such cases as Wolf's and included many ex-prisoners itself. The VONS network was inextricably connected with the Charter 77, and as both were now involved in the opposition movement, I did not expect to make much practical headway at Civic Forum.

I was surprised by the relaxed and low-key atmosphere of the Civic Forum office. I had imagined a throng of inquirers: there was a small knot of people. The staff all seemed to be of student age, smiling, casual, obliging; and if I was reminded of anything, it was of a university common room or a union office—an air of precarious organization. The word you were tempted to use—I thought of the hand-written posters and the single, small-screen televisions relaying information to potential crowds of hundreds—was 'amateur'. You had to remind yourself that a month ago the machinery of opposition and free information simply hadn't existed; and that, at a deeper level, all revolutions must appear to be started by amateurs.

Furthermore, if these were the amateurs, who were the professionals? No doubt, when the communist leaders were first compelled to negotiate with Civic Forum they must have stifled the thought (it was creepily instructive to have shared it) that the situation was preposterous—they were dealing with amateurs. But were they themselves professional in anything other than their official possession of power? Professional, in terms of expertise, responsibility, knowledge, capacity? The answer I got to this was to be repeatedly and vehemently 'No'. The constant cry—with a gush of relief now that at last it could be uttered openly—was that in a totalitarian regime stupidity floats to the top. At every level, control had passed for years into the hands of people with no qualification other than their Party allegiance. What Czechoslovakia desperately needs now is intelligence.

Jiří Wolf's name struck no immediate chords at Civic Forum. We asked after several of the names we had, some of them VONS people. Yes, one or two had been here, but they had gone. There was a little further conferring among the reception staff. Then someone disappeared and came back with a piece of paper. On it was written Wolf's name and a Prague telephone number. As simple as that.

It was well into the evening but we went to Alžběta's office and phoned the number. No answer. We tried several times. Meanwhile we talked and Alžběta studied the PEN dossier I had given her. It was clear that she had not fully appreciated how central to my visit was the search for Wolf, but she was becoming rapidly involved in it. We had a phone number, and it was perhaps now a straightforward matter. But there was a puzzlement which Alžběta shared. Why had she never heard of this man? And why had so many people, many of them on the circuits of information, at best only vague knowledge of him?

As we left the office and walked to get a meal, I began to feel that Wolf was having a distinct psychological effect on Alžběta— on top of all the emotion that the present crisis had brought. Here was a man whose painful history had been unknown to her only days before, and here was the prospect that soon many other such secrets must come to light. I did not imagine for one moment that Alžběta did not know of, better than I, the things that had been perpetrated in her country. But the individual case was acting, rightly or wrongly, as a catalyst to the assimilation of events.

As we walked, she spoke of things which do not often get mentioned in the West. How Charter 77 was in many ways, for all its courage and worthiness, an élitist and divisive body, exerting a tacit reproach against those who did not sign it, and throwing up within itself an inner circle of eminence at the expense of many an 'ordinary' signatory. It is generally true that in the West reference to Charter 77 evokes a handful of names. One forgets, firstly, that even by 1980 Charter 77 had more than a thousand signatories, and, secondly, that its total number of signatories was only ever a tiny proportion of the population. Alžběta was gently scoffing of those now flocking to sign the Charter. She also spoke of the pressurizing that had surrounded the signing of other petitions, such as that for the release of Havel; of a contagious attitude of 'if you are not for us, you are against us', which she pointed out was exactly the stance of the Communist Party.

What Alžběta was revealing was perhaps the inevitable nervousness and complexity that follow the simple, inspiring and hardly believable fact of revolutionary action. You could see the mechanisms of suspicion and trust, immunity and risk, rivalry and resentment beginning to turn themselves inside out: how good a non-communist were you? Old, familiar emotions were starting to flow stickily in a new direction.

I phoned the Wolf number that night. No answer. The next morning I tried again: same result. Alžběta had arranged a mid-morning meeting with Ludvík Vaculík; I was to go to her office first. I phoned Miloš to say we had Wolf's number and would keep trying it. Miloš was tied up for the day anyway. I then phoned a contact at the British Embassy Cultural Section to ask if someone could keep phoning the Wolf number through the morning. I then went to Alžběta's office on Národní Street.

Alžběta had had no luck with the Wolf number either. We tried again from her office without success, then walked to the Café Slavia at the far end of Národní Street to meet Vaculík.

Vaculík is a short, rather leonine-featured man in his sixties, with a thick, grey moustache and long, thick, grey hair. He is perhaps best known abroad for his novel *The Guinea Pigs*, written after the Soviet invasion, but his best work is considered to be *The Axe*, published before 1968. For a long time his work has been largely confined to essays, necessarily published in foreign and *emigré* journals. He is currently busy with volumes of diaries and correspondence. He remains one of Czechoslovakia's leading literary figures.

I had been warned that he was difficult, 'morose', that he might react contrarily to questions. In fact he was amiable, humorous, freely gave me his time and insisted on paying for the drinks. Vaculík rejected communism in the 1960s, but desribed himself as having had a 'lasting battle' with communism ever since he joined the Party. The Soviet invasion and subsequent crack-down meant the virtual loss of all previous freedoms. He spoke of his disbelief and despair at the time; a feeling—echoed by others I spoke to—that his life was lost, that the effects of the invasion would last and that he would not live (he gave a wry smile) to see them end.

He was forbidden to publish in Czechoslovakia and endured a

kind of house arrest. His decision to publish regularly abroad was effectively a decision to be regularly interrogated, and, like so many Czechoslovaks, he was obliged to keep monthly appointments with the police. His refusal to do menial work led to the threat of criminal proceedings for 'parasitism', though the charge was never brought. He had lost his pension rights, and he had no recourse to the assistance normally available for treatment following a gall-bladder operation. He was imprisoned once, for two days, for signing a petition to nominate Jaroslav Seifert for the Nobel Prize.

How did he view present developments?

He was a 'sceptical optimist'.

Was he bitter, did he regard the past as an evil joke?

No, it had to be viewed as a great, if terrible, lesson for world history and it should not be vulgarized.

How did he see the future?

There were two futures: one before and one after elections. Elections in the spring of 1990 seemed to him a reasonable possibility, with time enough to form parties and find personalities to stand.

Would he wish to stand himself?

No, it was his 'secret wish' to have nothing to do with politics.

In this last, frank admission Vaculík belied the stereotype of the Czechoslovak writer and perhaps expressed the inner feeling of many of his fellow authors. He exuded the dignified desire to protect his own independence. Our discussion moved on to the Czech Writers' Union, even then being denounced as a restrictive organ of the State. Vaculík, of course, was not a member, but nor did he wish to join the new free writers' association that was being formed. The scepticism in his optimism was apparent and even extended to some reservations about Civic Forum.

Did he think the perpetrators of repression should be punished?

An emphatic yes. But the punishment should be by law, not in the spirit of revenge, and those accused should include not only those responsible for the persecutions and imprisonments but those who had wreaked economic and environmental damage. One might need to accept that the punishment would not

19

correspond to the guilt, since the degree of criminality might never be properly determined.

What of the punishment for those personally involved in his own suffering?

Here Vaculík's individuality reasserted itself. He would like, he said, with a slyly wistful expression, to invite a certain police officer to his home, just as that police officer had issued many invitations to him. No one else, no publicity. A simple invitation to coffee.

Finally I asked Vaculík if he knew about Wolf. Once again, there was the vague recognition of the name, but he could not help me further.

After lunch I called in at the Cultural Section of the British Embassy. Had they got an answer from the Wolf number? Yes.

Would Saturday morning be all right for a meeting?

Mr Wolf couldn't give a precise time as yet, but would call back. And he only spoke Czech.

I was amazed. My goal appeared to have been achieved in less than twenty-four hours. And, with all my readiness to pursue numerous Czech contacts, it was a section of the British Embassy that had made the connection. I was still baffled. How had he sounded on the phone? Was he genuinely ready to meet or perhaps a little cautious?

Oh, perfectly ready, perfectly positive about it all. And he sounded fine.

As it happened, I was able to hear for myself. They had forgotten to give the number he should ring at the Section, so a further call was made to him, in Czech of course. The voice I overheard issuing from the receiver was business-like and robust. One image I had of Jiří Wolf, as a man physically and mentally wrecked and beyond rehabilitation, faded.

Back at the hotel, I phoned Miloš to tell him the news. Would he be free to act as interpreter?

Only if the meeting was early. Could it be on Friday instead—he had the whole day free?

I said Wolf had to choose the time. I could probably find

someone else for Saturday. It looked as if I might never get to meet Miloš.

This was late afternoon on Thursday the seventh. There had been stories during the day that Adamec, the prime minister, was threatening to resign. A stalemate seemed to have been reached between Civic Forum and the government. Civic Forum wanted a reformed government (with a non-communist majority) by Sunday, otherwise the general strike would go ahead. Adamec's position was that he would reform the government but would not act under pressure and ultimatums. If they continued, he would resign. Since Adamec was, temporarily at least, a significant figure in negotiations for both sides, this was not a desirable outcome.

Alžběta had arranged a further meeting with another writer, Eda Kriseova, that evening between six and seven. Kriseova spoke English and would come to the hotel, but I was not to be surprised if she did not show up. I fully expected her not to appear, since she was closely involved with Civic Forum and was currently privy to discussions with the government. But she was also a writer, and perhaps sometimes it is true that writers like to meet writers. At six o'clock she phoned from the lobby, and, though we could have talked in the hotel, we hurried across the street to a café.

Obviously in a hurry and excited, but smiling and genial, she was the first person I met who seemed truly charged with the electricity of events. She was also the first person to convey a real shiver of fear. She had been on a tram just now and people were saying that Adamec had resigned. If this had happened, then everything was thrown into flux. There would be a 'constitutional crisis'. There might be a 'putsch'. She used this word several times, as if she had not chosen it thoughtlessly.

This was unsettling, to say the least. I shared the generally accepted view that the way ahead for Civic Forum was not easy but that the current of change was essentially irreversible. Correspondents in the Western press at least were ruling out intervention by the army. But Kriseova seemed convinced it was still possible. 'I don't see many uniforms about,' I said rather obtusely, remembering that a year ago it was hard to get away from them.

'Exactly,' she said. 'Where *are* they all?'

It was hard to get the measure of Kriseova. She seemed both to have acquired a special grip on events (given her closeness to the centre of things, you could not deny her privileged viewpoint) and to have lost some normal hold on them. She herself seemed to acknowledge this. Her language had a heightened, even ecstatic quality. She spoke of the 'existential' nature of recent experience, of being 'on a wave' and having no choice, of something working 'through her', of events moving so fast that you were 'racing after history'. She also admitted to an uncanny sense of being involved in the unreal, to having asked her old friend, Havel: 'Václav, are we dreaming this? Are we acting this?'

The question reverberates. Theatrical metaphors need to be applied with care to Czechoslovakia where the theatre has traditionally involved itself very concretely in politics. It is no bizarre accident that the opposition movement was inaugurated by an actor (famous for his romantic leads), threw up as its protagonist a playwright, Václav Havel, and had its first headquarters in a theatre, the fantastically named 'Laterna Magica'. Yet here was Kriseova testifying to the actual feeling, as the Civic Forum leaders met inside a theatre, that surely they were in a play. No doubt all remarkable events may seem at first unreal, especially when they have the weight of twenty years to deny their possibility. For me too these days in Prague had an unreal tinge. But surely people *make* history, they don't act it (otherwise everything is excused). Nor do they run after it. Or do they?

Rapt as she seemed capable of being, Kriseova was full of earthy warmth and vitality, and she plainly had a bent for the practical. She described herself as Havel's 'fairy godmother', making sure, amid everything, that he got his medicine for the lung problems he has had since contracting pneumonia in prison. She was also, one guessed, a courageous woman. She spoke of the demonstration on the night of the seventeenth, at which she, her daughter and some five thousand others had been caught in the trap formed by the police in Národní Street, preventing access to Wenceslas Square. All sorts of accounts were circulating about this night. Some said that the police had been specially drugged; that they had used nets to snare small clusters of people; that bodies were seen lying under covers (this apart from the publicized rumour, later proved false, that a student had been killed).

What seemed beyond dispute was the ferocity of the police attacks and that this was a premeditated plan, executed to prevent the escape of a mass of people from a confined space. A public investigation (that unprecedented thing) was currently being conducted into the brutality. A neurologist had testified that the cases of shock were similar to those he had seen in people who had experienced bombardment in the war. Others pointed out that from the sheer weight of numbers and from crushing and confinement alone, fatalities would have been likely.

Absolutely beyond doubt is that 17 November was a turning-point in events and a colossal mistake by the authorities. The world changed overnight.

Like Vaculík, Kriseova had found herself stripped of hope in 1969. Formerly a successful journalist, she suddenly had nothing, and had to wrench herself from despair. She took work in a mental hospital, which she says saved her from going mad herself. She saw that the inmates were 'free' in a way those outside were not. Her first stories arose from her mental hospital experience. In the seventies she came under scrutiny and threats from the security police and after refusing to 'retract' had established, like Vaculík, a regular 'relationship' with an investigator and was, of course, prevented from publishing.

How did she get involved in Civic Forum?

She had once presciently told Havel that if he ever got drawn into things so much that he needed help, he should call her. He called soon after.

Was she bitter about the 'lost' years and did she want retribution?

You had to remember, she said, that the worst time was in the fifties. The generation that had known that time was conditioned by its terrible memories, numbed into submission. Even now many of them were sceptical. The generations of the sixties and after had not lost their hope. And you had to get retribution into perspective: one woman who had been assaulted at night in the street was found screaming, 'They are killing us now! They are going to kill us!' Her assailant was a solitary molester but the woman was a Party member and genuinely feared an opposition massacre.

The Prague streets did indeed seem a little darker after speaking to Kriseova. In the café the talk had been confirmed: Adamec had stepped down. But even as she hurried to a possible constitutional crisis, Kriseova was making arrangements to meet me again, to give me some of her stories. I must read them, we must discuss them. Writers!

At the hotel there were no messages about Wolf. I phoned Alžběta to tell her that we seemed to have a meeting with Wolf on Saturday. Could she possibly be there to interpret? I also told her what Kriseova had said and discussed the evening's news. I could hear anxiety creeping into her voice. I could not tell if this arose from her own assessment of the situation or from my words, the garbled, intrusive words of a foreigner clumsily relaying inside information from one Czech to another. The palpable throb of rumour.

The next morning was bright and clear. There were no uniforms on the street and the trams were crossing the bridge over the Vltava as usual. I had to be at Alžběta's office at ten-thirty to meet Ivan Klíma. (Alžběta seemed to have abandoned normal work, but a revolution was a good excuse.) I phoned the Cultural Section to see if there was a definite time for Wolf.

We're glad you phoned, I was told. You see, the thing is, there's been a mistake. The man we spoke to phoned back and said that, after thinking it over, it seemed a little strange that you wanted to meet him. You see, the fact is, whoever he is, he's the wrong man. He's not Jiří Wolf.

I called Miloš. I let the enigma of the bogus Wolf go. It was Friday, Miloš's free day. We were back to where we started. He was at my service. He would do some scouting while I went to see Klíma. I also called a number of contacts I had neglected to follow up, believing we had found Wolf. These included a man called Hejda, a man called Freund and a man called Doruzka, a leading jazz figure (this a recommendation from Josef Škvorecký) who might put me on to a man called Srp [sic] who might know Wolf personally. Hejda didn't know about Wolf but suggested someone whom I had already tried without success. Freund was out but his wife said she would pass on a message. Doruzka, in stylishly idiomatic English, sounded the key-note of my search so far: 'No, I am afraid this man's name does not ring any bells with me.'

Now that Wolf was once again a mystery, I could not resist indulging in dubious theories. Could it be that Wolf, on his release, had simply wished to disappear? Could it be that there was something about his personality that had kept him removed from the main circles of activists? Had he always been, perhaps, a little mad? Some of the names and phone numbers I had were copied directly from a typed information sheet on a window in Národní Street, giving details about Pavel Wonka, who had died in prison the previous year. It seemed extraordinary that, if such matters were now public, Wolf should be so elusive.

I told myself that my hypotheses were indeed indulgent. It was wrong to construct riddles merely out of my lack of luck in finding a man. I went to Alžběta's office to see Klíma.

I had met Klíma on my previous visit. He is a tall, rather gangling man, with straggly dark hair, a sort of misshapen handsomeness and a crinkly smile. He has the air of a veteran from beatnik days and speaks good English. Popular at the time of the Prague Spring, mainly as a playwright, he now has a high reputation, both in and outside his country, as a novelist. Much of his work, though perhaps not the very best, has appeared in English. His untranslated *Soudce z Milosti* is considered, along with Vaculík's *The Axe*, to be one of the great Czechoslovak novels of recent times.

Comparatively speaking, Klíma has not been severely persecuted during the last twenty years, and I wondered whether for some this has slightly diminished his otherwise considerable standing. Despite the ban on his work at home, he has been able to survive on foreign royalties, to keep up a steady rate of production, and he emanated relative contentment. His life, on the other hand, has scarcely been easy. In 1969 he managed to visit an American university, leaving on the very day (31 August) before the borders were closed. His passport was confiscated on his return and he was not able to travel for eleven years, and then only within Eastern Europe. He ceased to write plays because of the impossibility of seeing them staged. He was harassed, his home searched, his telephone tampered with, but he was never arrested or imprisoned.

Klíma is neither complacent nor possessed of any false guilt at not being in the top league of the persecuted. He has a strong sense of his own individuality—I suspect that he shared Vaculík's 'secret wish' not to be involved in politics—and even a rather gleeful sense of irony about how his case goes against the grain of some received Western ideas. He pointed out that he did not sign Charter 77, but, as many of his friends were signatories and he moved in Charter circles, he was none the less subject to scrutiny. He also implied that not signing Charter 77 might have been a tactical advantage: you could be active without advertising the fact. He was not snubbed for not signing. His position was that as an author he wished to sign only his own texts.

Unlike Vaculík, Klíma did not disdain manual work. Rather, he took the view that doing other, temporary jobs could be valuable for a writer; and he told a story which was a perfect explosion of the Western 'myth'. A famous Czech author is seen cleaning the streets by a friend of his at the American Embassy. The American goes into a fit of outrage at how the authorities humiliate the country's best minds. But the writer (could it be Klíma?) is doing the job voluntarily: it is research for a book.

We discussed Havel, who conforms in paramount fashion to the Western myth and who at that moment was being tipped for president. There were two possible views of Havel in my mind. One, that he was a man moving willingly to meet his destiny as leader of the people; the other, that he was being sucked into events at some cost to himself, a writer uprooted from his true vocation.

But it seemed that Havel did not have the 'secret wish'. Klíma said that Havel was, of course, exhausted right now, but underneath he was happy. He called him a 'childish' man (I think he meant 'child-like'). He was happy to be the great citizen. He was a brave man, yes, but he had political ambitions—they were not thrust upon him. Klíma had always found Havel's essays and political writings more impressive than his plays.

We spoke of other Czech writers, the exiles Kundera and Škvorecký. Klíma thought Kundera was a great writer but self-interested. He played up to Western preconceptions in terms of both his own position and his portrayal of Czechoslovakia, which Klíma found often superficial and too eager for symbols. *The Unbearable Lightness of Being* was not entirely liked in Czechoslovakia. Škvorecký, on the other hand, retained a strong following, particularly among the younger generation, and was seen as the exile with the greater integrity.

We turned to Czechoslovak writing generally and to what the future held. Both Vaculík and Kriseova had spoken forcibly about the discrediting of the Czech Writers' Union, and Vaculík had wished to hold back even from the newly established free association of writers. Klíma seemed to be directly involved in the founding of this new association (*Obec*—'Community'), but some of the harshest language of a generally gently spoken man was reserved for the old Union. He called it an 'instrument of national treason' which for twenty years had accepted without protest that hundreds of Czech writers were suppressed and persecuted if not imprisoned. The Union, he said, was 'covered in shame.' However, there should be no 'craving for revenge.' Members of the old Union should be allowed, as individuals, to join the new Community. This was in accordance with the Community's overriding commitment to freedom of expression. But there was to be no 'fusion' between the two bodies.

What of the Union's money, its assets?

Klíma said, with some bitterness, that the Union had no assets, only tables and typewriters. Then he said there should be a calling to account for the 'abuse of literary funds'.

I half appreciated what he meant. I knew that all writers, Union members or not, were obliged to pay a percentage of income to a Literary Fund. In effect, writers who were banned were forced to pay for the privileges of the approved.

From my visit of the year before, I had a graphic illustration of what these privileges might entail. I vividly remember being taken from Bratislava on a snowy day to a 'castle' in the Slovak countryside, which was owned by, or rather allocated to, the Slovak Writers' Union. I have to say that those who took me did so in a spirit of hospitality but also with detectable unease.

The 'castle' was a grand country house, set in extensive grounds and approached along a magnificent avenue of poplars. I was told that for a very small payment writers could come here to work; though few of the many rooms seemed occupied. None the less, we were greeted by a permanent staff and ushered into a building that was as warmly heated as it was immaculately decorated and furnished. I was given a brief tour and shown one of the best bedrooms—one of the most sumptuous and elegant guest-rooms I have ever seen. Brezhnev, I was told, once slept here.

For their small payment, writers were also fed. There were only four of us, and the place really did seem empty, but a table (dwarfed by the proportions of the room around it) was laid for lunch, complete with fine cutlery and glassware. While snow fell outside on to noble trees, a waitress served us a meal worthy of any restaurant, in an atmosphere of Cinderella-like fantasy.

I asked Klíma what would become of such places and of the Literary Fund. He said the Literary Fund and all that it paid for—the 'castles', the Union buildings, offices, secretaries—all belonged to the Ministry of Culture. The Union owned nothing. He did not know what would happen now. He said that foreigners often overlooked the abuses in his country that were insidious and did not form neat or dramatic symbols. Of course individuals had been martyrs and suffered terribly and bravely, but the real damage was the gradual erosion of the self-respect of a whole people, the spread of corruption and the simultaneous ruination, by progressive mismanagement, of the economy and the environment.

It was perhaps the wrong moment, but I asked Klíma about Wolf.

No, Wolf's case was not familiar to him.

I lunched with Alžběta. I had told her about Wolf proving not to be Wolf. She seemed in a low mood. I was not sure if this was because she had entered the spirit of the search and felt thwarted or because she was anxious at the uncertainty still surrounding Adamec's resignation. Klíma had a theory that Adamec had resigned with the hidden purpose of popping up again as president. The ultimatum of the general strike stood. The streets were still calm. I went back to the hotel and waited for a call from Miloš.

Miloš duly rang, in positive mood. He had inquired again at

Civic Forum. No success. Then he had tracked down some VONS people and had been given an address for Wolf in Prague. No phone. He had gone to the address and found no one there. But he had left a note on the door, with a brief explanation, asking Wolf to call him or (if he spoke English) to call me at the hotel. So far, no replies. But we could only wait and see. I made a note of the address and we agreed to phone each other as soon as we heard anything.

I waited. The situation was a considerable improvement from the morning—at least I knew Wolf was in Prague. But, as time went by, I started to have doubts. Wolf did not have to be at the address at all. I also reflected on the wisdom of leaving notes on doors. Surely this was rash, even now. A forgotten fact came back to me: Wolf's sentence had included not only six years' imprisonment, now served, but also three years' subsequent 'protective surveillance'.

Late that evening there was a knock on my door. Surely not? No, it was Eda Kriseova, eyes bloodshot with fatigue, but smiling, dressed in a trench coat and chic black hat and clutching a folder of papers. The scene was straight out of a spy movie.

Would she like a drink?

No, she was too tired; she had been all day with Civic Forum; she had to go and rest. But here were the stories and extracts from a novel she had promised to bring me. We talked for a moment in the corridor. She told me that Civic Forum had reached provisional agreement for a reformed government and that President Husak would resign that weekend. I hardly registered the full import of these quietly spoken words. I took the folder and wished her good night.

Two things struck me. That despite what was clearly an exhausting and historic day, she was still writer enough to find time to bring me her manuscripts. Secondly, that this was one of Prague's 'international' hotels, much used by Western visitors, and three weeks ago one might legitimately have feared bugs and the ears of informers. But here was Kriseova announcing her momentous news in one of its corridors. Thus you learn of the fall of tyrants.

I began reading Kriseova's work immediately. The green light on my phone came on. Wolf? No. A message left by a Mr Freund, giving the same address for Wolf that Miloš had discovered.

It was snowing the next morning. I phoned Miloš, who had

heard nothing and would be busy until four o'clock. I had an arrangement to meet Igor from Bratislava at two in the hotel lobby. Miloš said he could find time to call me around one-thirty. The morning was free and, though I was beginning to lose hope, I resolved to go to Wolf's address myself on blind chance. Since this might have been fruitless anyway without someone who spoke Czech, I called Alžběta. If Kriseova was Havel's fairy godmother, Alžběta was surely the fairy godmother of my search for Wolf. It was Saturday, I could hear a child in the background, but she agreed to come.

By a stroke of luck, the address given for Wolf was not far from where Alžběta herself lived, south of the centre of Prague, some three stops on the metro from Wenceslas Square. Alžběta met me at the station and, following a street map, we walked through the snow. Wolf's street was a quiet cul-de-sac (though all the streets seemed quiet), with family houses on one side and a run-down apartment block, where Wolf lived, on the other. His door, with his name on it, was on the first floor. A cold, gloomy landing. We knocked. No answer.

Jammed in the door-frame was a pencil-written note on a scrap of paper, which, according to Alžběta, was to a woman and simply said, 'Wait for me here.' It seemed to have been written by Wolf himself and suggested he had been here recently. We knocked again, just in case, waited, considered; then knocked at a neighbour's along the landing. A burly man in a check shirt appeared, who did not seem unduly suspicious of us.

Yes, Wolf was around—he had seen him this morning. He had complained of not sleeping. Yes, he knew who Wolf was. Wolf was out and about a lot; he was still 'active', perhaps. Yes, my own son is with Charter 77.

Did Wolf look well?

He didn't look so bad.

We deliberated. Alžběta was for waiting; then for leaving a note. I was unsure. This would be the second note from a stranger on his door in twenty-four hours. I was beginning to think that the truth of the matter was that, whatever Wolf was doing now, he did not want intrusion; perhaps he should be left alone. And I was beginning to question my persistence in seeking him out—the whole absurd folly of a Western visitor trying to find an elusive Czech dissident. Was I not conducting a grotesque parody of the 'protective surveillance' that, for all I knew, Wolf was still subject to? I had got carried away with the detective-hunt element of things and had somehow pushed to the back of my mind the terrible facts that had provoked my interest in the first place. As though merely finding him mattered!

Alžběta left a note, this time giving her phone number as a further point of contact. We walked back to the metro in a subdued mood. I would probably not see Alžběta again before I left. She was sorry that with all our efforts we had not met with success. The search had led us only to mutual self-searching.

At the hotel there were no messages. Igor was due shortly. I looked forward to his arrival. I had called him from Prague at a point when I illusorily believed that my task would be accomplished by Saturday afternoon: the time would be free. I would have to explain what had happened, but I felt the situation was essentially unchanged: I had done all I could. Just before I met Igor, Miloš phoned, as promised. No further news. I explained that I had been to Wolf's address myself and that my feeling now was that Wolf was a man who wanted to keep to himself.

'No, no,' said Miloš, with some emphasis, 'my information about him is that he would not find this intrusive; he would be ready to meet.

I wrote a note for the reception desk, saying that if I had any callers or visitors, especially a Mr Wolf, I would be back at six. Then I waited in the lobby for Igor. He showed up, wearing the badge of Civic Forum's Slovak sister movement, People Against Violence, and we went off to a café on the Old Town Square. We intended to take a walk across the river to Hradčany, but the weather was bitter and, with much to talk about, we were still sitting there at five.

Igor's presence was a reminder of the elementary fact that Czechoslovakia is a federation of two states, the Czech and the Slovak. The negotiations to reform the government, going on even as we spoke, involved a good deal of juggling of Slovak against Czech as well as communist against non-communist representation. The Slovaks are proud of their Slovakness—in Igor's company you learn not to use the word 'Czech' to apply to the country as a whole. But Igor was generally sceptical of the notion that political changes might lead to an awkward upsurge of Slovak nationalism.

Events in Bratislava appeared to have run a parallel course to those in Prague, with the Bratislavs having the particular excitement of being suddenly allowed to travel freely across the Austrian border, less than five miles away. In practice, Czechs and Slovaks are still restrained from foreign travel by the lack of foreign money. But here was a chance to to-and-fro across a ghostly Iron Curtain just for the sake of it, East Berliner style, several return trips a day.

Were there any problems peculiar to Slovakia?

Yes, eastern Slovakia was a notoriously 'remote' part of the country and the spread of information from the capital had proved difficult, meeting with confusion and distrust. (Vaculík and Kriseova had made the same point about the rural areas generally). The authorities seemed to have colluded in the problem, since there was a remarkable incidence of power-cuts at the same time as opposition broadcasts. But not all Igor's stories raised laughter. There was the one about the Russian soldier (the Soviet army was still there of course, keeping a *very* low profile) found hanged near a railway station. Suicide? Or something else?

At five-thirty we walked back to the hotel. Igor was good company. My pensive mood of the morning had lifted and I was now sanguinely resigned to the fact that I would not meet Wolf. When we entered the lobby I could see there was a message for me next to my key. It said: 'I am tall with bushy hair and glasses. I am waiting in the lounge. When you read this Mr Wolf will probably be waiting too. Miloš.'

I am still confused as to how this small miracle occurred: whether Wolf and Miloš converged on the hotel by mutual arrangement or by some remarkable coincidence. Even after later hearing Miloš's account, I am not entirely sure of the exact sequence of events.

I walked, with Igor, round the corner into the lounge. There was Miloš, as described. There, introduced by him, was Wolf. And there was a third man, who spoke English and gave his name as Weiss. We moved to another part of the lounge which could accommodate us all, and the whole strange, short encounter began.

The first element of strangeness was the setting. To repeat, this was one of Prague's big hotels. It was a Saturday evening. The lounge was busy and hung with Christmas decorations. We might have gone to my room, or somewhere else, the choice was Wolf's; but we were sitting down to talk in a place that only recently would have been quite unsafe, and perhaps still was. I was conscious throughout that people *were* listening to us (who would not have eavesdropped?). I vividly recall the young waiter, with the face of a bespectacled sixth-former, who brought our drinks and stared boggle-eyed, transfixed by what Wolf was saying.

A second element of strangeness was the air of feverish, if business-like haste. From the moment he sat down, Wolf launched into a monologue, interrupted almost exclusively by Miloš's disciplined translations. There were no questions put to me about the nature of my interest and no opportunity for me to explain it voluntarily. Nor was there much opportunity for me to ask questions. The nearest thing to small talk came from Weiss, who was the third element of strangeness. I had not anticipated a mystery companion, though such a figure should not have been so unexpected. It became plain that Weiss was not just there for his English; he was looking after Wolf in some way. He said of Wolf at one point: 'He is part of my family now.' It emerged that Weiss had been a prisoner too, for several years, some of them in Valdice.

The contrast between Weiss and Wolf could scarcely have been more pronounced. Whereas Wolf was all contained nervous energy and concentration, Weiss was relaxed, smiled a lot and was ready, when he could, even to joke and digress. He apologized for his teeth, which had been damaged in prison, but the defect hardly marred a kindly, avuncular face. Weiss was dressed in a casual cardigan; Wolf in a suit and tie which, if it were not for a general dishevelment (the tie was quickly loosened), might have been called dapper. The clothes had been sent from America.

In the space of an hour, I learned a little about Weiss, the man:

that his passions were airplanes, that he had a library of eight thousand books. I learned very little about Wolf. When Wolf said that his wife had divorced him because she did not wish to be married to a criminal, there was no emotion and the remark was made almost incidentally. Weiss chipped in that his wife too had divorced him when he was a prisoner, but, on his release, they had met up again and married for the second time; and he was evidently delighted to repeat the story. It was as though Weiss was there to give the picture of a man who had been a prisoner yet was restored to a benign, rounded humanity.

Wolf was short, with the sort of slight frame that often suggests an intense mental life. Afterwards, when I asked myself the question, 'If you hadn't known who Wolf was, what would you have taken him for?' I answered: I would have taken him for some *distrait* chess-player, an obsessive academic, a mathematician. His face was distinctly Jewish, and I wondered how this may have affected the treatment he received from prison guards. He blinked a lot, with a twitch to his cheek, a definite tic. He sat on my right, with Miloš to my left. He spoke rapidly, a little breathlessly, mostly looking straight ahead or at Miloš, but now and then turning to me with a sort of uncertain smile, which I rightly or wrongly took as a seeking of reassurance. His hands were in contrast to the rest of him: thick, blunt fingers, with very little spare nail.

What did he say? In one sense he said what I had already heard, since the substance of his monologue, elaborated and extended, was similar to that of the dossier I had read on him and covered much the same ground. It was the third-person, case-history Wolf of the dossier, rather than the direct, first-person, intensely pitiable Wolf of the prison writings. There was, of course, something utterly new and strange in hearing facts already half-known issuing from the lips of the man himself. But I confess to more than once having the absurd urge to stop him and say, 'I think I know this. Tell me about *yourself.*'

There was also the sense that what he was uttering was prepared, rehearsed, had often been repeated. He had certain things to say, then he would finish. It did not take long to surmise that Wolf had probably been doing a lot of this recently. Telling a lot of different people or groups of people, if rarely stray visitors from

England, the facts. This was his work now, his task, the way in which, according to his neighbour, he was still 'active'. It was also, at some deeper level, the way he wanted, and was able, to deal with things. Weiss later confirmed the intuition. He said, 'We are very busy politically.' He spoke of fears that the prisons would be slow to change, that there would be a conspiracy to destroy prison and court records, a general hushing-up.

The repeated note from Wolf was forensic and legalistic: the attestation to accumulated injustice. He was not interested in his 'human story', nor in sensation, nor, save when he referred to Czechoslovakia's 'Gulag', in rhetoric. When he stated that he had received ten days of solitary confinement and a halving of rations for having a loose button, and I had to ask him, in amazement, to repeat what he had said, he did not dwell on the matter. When he remarked that a 'co-defendant' had been released after one year and was working 'to this day' for the state security, it was spoken without special stress or elaboration, like the reference to his divorce.

His release on 17 May had been at the full term of his prison sentence. He had been ill for a month and was treated by a neurologist. Necessary follow-up treatment proved unforthcoming, partly because doctors were afraid of his reputation with the secret police. When fit to do so, he was required to report to the police every day. There were problems with both employment and accommodation, and there was pressure on him to leave Prague.

He was held in custody twelve times after he was released that spring, with a flurry of detentions in August. Court proceedings were opened against him twice. The police entered his flat several times, sometimes at night. The last such visit was on 15 November, less than three weeks ago. In the same month, when he was working as a stoker in a boiler-room, he was visited by police who threatened to throw him into the furnace. On 17 November he was arrested at home and held till eleven that night to prevent his participation in the events of that day. Since 17 November he has refused to go to a police station, but since the seventeenth (the finality of that day!) persecution of him has ceased.

Wolf spoke of his years in prison with the intent but impersonal tone of a man in a witness box. There was little actual description. In ten years, prison rations were cut by half, but the work-loads of enforced labour were increased. Prisoners were required to *pay* for their maintenance in prison, but because of reductions in their wages for forced labour and because of other financial penalties, the 'bill' could never be met. Wolf is still technically in debt to the state for 4,200 crowns for the privilege of six years' brutal punishment.

Conditions for political prisoners were worse than for others, one aspect of their degradation being that they were thrown in with the worst criminals (Weiss's foreman at one time was a triple murderer). Political prisoners were selected for the worst work and were not allowed to associate with each other. They were subjected to close scrutiny of their behaviour and speech and to regular reports by warders, who were directed to destroy prisoners psychologically. All prison functionaries, medical staff as well as guards, colluded in the cover-up of breaches of law and human rights.

Wolf was manifestly a brave man, but his readiness to endure the worst showed a staggering single-mindedness. When his half-sister asked for remission for him, Wolf refused to sign the application, on the grounds that only those who were guilty could ask for remission: accepting remission amounted to retraction. When he received his six-year sentence he also refused to appeal, on the grounds that he did not accept the legality of the verdict. He annulled an appeal made on his behalf by a lawyer. Pressure was put on him to bring an appeal, to demonstrate the fairness of the courts, and he was promised one year off his sentence. Wolf did not comply. In the twenty-two months interval, between his two stretches of imprisonment, Wolf had been offered political asylum in France. He had refused on the grounds that, if he were granted asylum, all *other* political victims should be offered the same.

After making this last point, Wolf brought things to an abrupt close. I had been wondering how long he would continue, whether there would be a more flexible stage in which he would be open to question. But now he gave a quick expulsion of breath, said something which I was sure was the Czech equivalent to 'That's it', and made the knee-patting gesture of a man about to depart. I looked at Igor, who looked bemused, and at Miloš, who wore his interpreter's mask. There was a reaching for coats, some final hand-shaking, some pleasantries from Weiss, and then the two were gone, as if hastening to some other, similar appointment, leaving behind them a vacuum of bewilderment and the consciousness that all around us were eyes and ears.

Why should I have been so stunned? Given Wolf's history, I had been ready for anything, so why was the reality so confounding? And why, beneath it all, did I have a perverse feeling of disappointment? I had met him; he had spoken, on his own terms, which were the only proper terms; I had listened. Why should I feel sorry if I felt I was nowhere nearer to knowing the man? What right did I have to know him? If I could conceive at all of what ten years of his kind of imprisonment might take away from a man, how should I expect anything to be rendered to me in an hour?

I had never asked him about his writing. What happened to that earlier work? Confiscated, destroyed? Did he (absurd question somehow) still want to write? It was ironic that I had met three other writers who, each with their own personal nuance, had transcended the image of the 'suffering Czech', yet Wolf had given it back to me in hard, annunciatory fact, as if at a press conference, with scarcely a touch of the personal.

Miloš had to leave. I thanked him for all he had done. Igor and I had a strong desire to be out of the hotel. As we walked off, I, for one, could not resist looking over my shoulder. We began the process of analyzing what we had just experienced, but this slid into the anaesthetic urge to find a restaurant that served Slovak food, to drink several glasses of vodka, followed by several glasses of wine. A radio was switched on in the restaurant. It confirmed what Kriseova had told me in the hotel corridor: a new government would be sworn in tomorrow; the president would resign. It was the end of an era.

Walking late that night across the lower end of Wenceslas Square, I was stopped, not by a secret policeman, nor by a celebrating citizen, but by a street huckster with a small, puckered, toothless face. I thought my English would deter him, but he grabbed my hand, studied my palm and, with a confident American twang, assessed my life and character as follows: I had been a naughty boy, oh yes, a very naughty boy; and I would live to be seventy-four. This cost me ten crowns.

My last morning in Prague—Sunday the tenth, the day communist domination would cease—bloomed brilliant and clear. A huge rally was planned for the afternoon in Wenceslas Square when the new government would be announced. But I had to be at the airport at two, and in any case had the feeling I would be an intruder at someone else's party. On my last day I wanted to do what I had not yet done: to cross the river, to walk up the Hradčany, to the castle, and appreciate that Prague is beautiful. A year ago the beauty had seemed bogus, even sinister. What place did aesthetics have in politics? But now, perhaps, Prague could be truly, unashamedly beautiful again. And so it was, its valleys and crests of architecture rising out of the dazzle of the winter morning.

Igor came with me. We crossed the Charles Bridge, seagulls squawking around us. What place did aesthetics have in politics? Seifert, whose love of Prague was as fierce as it was gentle, and who did not live, like Vaculík, to see the end of repression, wrote, with his own terrible heed of aesthetics:

> *When I shall die—and this will be quite soon—*
> *I shall still carry in my heart*
> *this city's destiny.*
>
> *And mercilessly, just as Marsyas,*
> *let anyone be flayed alive*
> *who lays hands on this city,*
> *no matter who he is,*
> *no matter how sweetly he plays*
> *on his flute.*

The Czechoslovak people, the guide-books say, have always honoured their writers. The road up to the castle is named after a writer, the poet Jan Neruda, from whom Pablo Neruda borrowed his name. Hunched against the castle walls is the impossibly tiny, fairy-tale house where Kafka wrote part of *The Trial*. And all over Prague there were poems, of a kind, blossoming on walls and windows and statues. Someone will anthologize them, if they haven't already. Igor translated: 'Husak, you talked a lot, but you said nothing.' 'He has eyes but he does not see; he has ears but he does not hear: who is he?'

Writers, writers!

We walked through the courtyards of the Presidential Palace, where even at that hour, perhaps, Husak was enjoying or suffering his last lunch as president, and over which flew the presidential flag with its motto which, on this day, could not have been more ironic, more Delphically barbed: 'Truth Shall Win.'

Igor insisted on coming to the airport to see me off. With events just beginning on Wenceslas Square, this seemed a considerable sacrifice. Perhaps he shared the 'secret wish'. Did Wolf have— would he, could he, ever have that wish?

Later, on the phone, Igor told me he had gone back and caught the last of it: he 'couldn't resist.'

A television in the airport concourse showed pictures of the jubilant crowds. The plane left on time, minutes after the president's resignation. There were several Czechoslovaks on board and I wondered how they felt, to be flying out of their country on the day of its deliverance.

Overleaf: Jiří Wolf, the Continental Hotel, 9 December

NEAL ASCHERSON
THE BORDERLANDS

You did not engrave yourself into popular memory, Byelorussia. You did not confiscate the liberty of others or plunder foreign lands or murder people who came from beyond your neighbour's furrow. You gave to strangers respect and the cake of hospitality; you gave to robbers your last cow and the last crumb of rye bread with the sign of the Cross . . . When I remember Byelorussian words, when the wind blows from the north-east, when I see a linen shirt with that sad embroidery, when I hear a cry of pain which does not blame . . . then I always feel the sudden chill of vague accusations of conscience, a sense of shared guilt and of shame. Byelorussia, Byelorussia, grey-green with a huge sky over your faded head, you are too good and gentle and generous for our times.

Tadeusz Konwicki, *The Calendar and the Hourglass*

Here is the forest. Not just a forest, but a *puszcza*: a Polish word that means a world of trees which have never been felled since the first bands of human beings arrived to hunt here. The *Puszcza* of Kniszyn, which begins north-east of the Polish city of Białystok, must be ten thousand years old.

To reach the village of Lipowy Most, I set off from the city Białystok along the road which leads to the Soviet frontier. I turned off the tarred highway at the spot where an oak tree grows upon a mound, a tree on which the Russians hanged Polish insurgents during the January Rising of 1863. That is to say: the vain Polish insurrection for independence which began in January but which lasted for fifteen months—for even longer, in the *puszcza*.

The road to the village is made of sand and dust. It ends in a wide clearing, large enough for fields of rye and a cluster of wooden houses. The history of this village began in 1918, when the three empires which had partitioned Poland between them for 123 years—Russia, Germany and Austria—collapsed almost simultaneously. Poland stood up among the ruins and reclaimed its independence, and the new government decided to honour a man, by then old, who had fought for the nation in 1863. It gave him this land for his six sons, and their descendants are still here. But the

43

government also intended, by settling veteran patriots and their children on this land, to post more sentries along what the Poles consider to be the eastern frontier of Europe— the *przedmurze* (bastion) of the Catholic West.

Lipowy Most is still a Catholic village. But the peasants who inhabit other clearings in this forest are not Catholic: they are Russian Orthodox. They, the original inhabitants, are Slavs but neither Russian nor Polish. They are Byelorussians.

- The forest edge is a few hundred yards away from the village, past two wooden crosses wreathed with herbs and rowan. Deer, lynx and boar live here, beavers and wolves and—further south—a few bison. I am sitting on a bench with my back against one of the houses, at the end of a summer day, doing nothing more than inhaling: sorting out the scents and tasting each, like a dog. The smells from the forest itself—pine-needles and resin, heather, sphagnum moss, the whiff of boletus mushrooms, moist earth—mix with wood-smoke, trodden rowan berries, long grass heated by the sun, cooking in one of the cottages, a dish of apples. It is entirely silent. Then a voice echoes against the forest wall and dies away.

How would a shot resound, a shot fired deep in the forest by a survivor from an invading army or a partisan band, by somebody who had stayed among the trees and never given in? Through the door of one of these huts, they carried young men wounded in the 1863 Insurrection. The Home Army resistance fought the Nazis here, and some of its detachments fought on against the Communist government long after the war. A few armed men remained in this forest, so the villagers say, until 1957. Kazimierz Brandys wrote a short story called 'The Bear' about a partisan man who wouldn't come out of the trees. In the end he lost his shape, became a tale to scare children, a shadow at dawn near the forest edge, the booming echoes of a rifle-shot heard between dreaming and starting awake.

The children of a Białystok doctor, here for the summer holidays, spend their days exploring in the forest. On the wall of the barn, they hang the helmets they find. Two German ones, rusted and pierced. Today the boy found a Red Army helmet, not much corroded, which he spotted lying half-buried in the bank of a stream. Patriots, bandits, fugitives and their pursuers, Scottish mercenaries, Swedish musketeers from the Great Northern War,

Russians and Germans, all have fallen here and disintegrated into the moss. I know a man who went mushrooming and found, in a distant clearing, the wreck of a French supply-wagon from the 1812 Retreat from Moscow, with Grande Armée buttons scattered around it. The *puszcza* has been swallowing the dead for many centuries.

There are also mass graves in the *puszcza*, where the skeletons lie face-down in rows, their hands bound behind them with barbed wire. North of here, they are digging into the sandy forest floor at Giby, where they know that anti-communist Poles and Home Army men were murdered in 1945. They have found corpses, but so far they are all German soldiers. The women of Giby have dreams; they give new directions to the diggers.

I have been reporting from Poland, on and off, for more than thirty years. But I had never before come to this north-eastern corner of Poland, wedged up against the borders of the Soviet republics of Lithuania and Byelorussia. Białystok was a town on the way to nowhere else, not specially historic, not a perch for brilliant minds. I knew that non-Polish minorities lived round here: Lithuanians and Byelorussians whose ancient territory had been transected by the frontier. But I also knew that they lived under such close surveillance by the Party authorities and the security police that it would be a long job getting them to talk.

Then, in the summer of 1989, Poland became the centre of the world, as it had been exactly fifty years before. World War Two began here; now the Cold War, perhaps even the Bolshevik Revolution itself, was ending here. The communist era of Polish history was over. In June, there were the first even semi-free elections to be held in the Soviet zone of Europe for forty years. Two years before, a few crazy optimists predicted that the Soviet Union might tolerate such an event early in the twenty-first century.

The end came suddenly. After the second wave of strikes in 1988, General Jaruzelski and his prime minister Mieczysław Rakowski surrendered. They summoned a round-table meeting of opposition and régime, of Solidarity leaders and those who had recently been their gaolers. Sessions began early in 1989. Decisions came rapidly. Solidarity was re-legalized, and 'free' elections were announced. Their freedom was qualified because the electoral law included a quota of reserved seats, designed to guarantee that the Communists—Polish United Workers' Party—had a majority in the Sejm, the lower house of parliament.

But the June elections produced a vote of universal, merciless hatred against the candidates of the United Workers' Party and the Communist-led 'coalition'. Almost every regime name that the voter could identify was crossed out. Nobody, not even Solidarity, had expected such a devastating result. The regime began to come apart, the satellite parties defected and sought alliance with Solidarity and the round-table deal (which had foreseen Solidarity only as a 'constructive opposition') swiftly unravelled. On 13 September, Tadeusz Mazowiecki formed the first essentially non-communist government in Warsaw since 1945.

These were extraordinary weeks to be in Poland, and yet weeks weirdly lacking passion. I thought at first that I had grown too cynical for joy, but then I found that Poles, too, seemed to feel that this couldn't really be happening. There was little exaltation, no visions: none of the intensity I remembered from the weeks in the Lenin Shipyard in 1980 or during the first visit of this Pope to his homeland in 1979. From the balcony of the Sejm, I looked down in serene disbelief at people I had known as fugitives, martyrs and revolutionaries, now sprawling on the benches or darting to the tribune as if they had been parliamentarians all their lives: Jacek Kuroń, Adam Michnik, Janek Lityński, Janusz Onyszkiewicz.

A year ago, these were still people who always ate when they sat down. They would hurry into the clandestine committee meeting, throw themselves into a chair and—in a single movement—pull from their brief-cases leaflets, typed reports, bread and sausage. They would eat mouthfuls between reading paragraphs about underground cells in the Ursus tractor plant. Then they would gulp a glassful of tea, grab a cigarette and be on their way. In the cool white corridor of the Sejm, one of them said to me: 'Now I'm the honourable member for S . . . But when we take our seats and Jacek starts speaking, I still feel my belly rumbling.'

I first went to Białystok in June 1989, to see the climax of the
election campaign. In the park, there was a Solidarity mass rally
with the candidates, pop groups, the cabaret star Jan Pietrzak.
The whole town seemed to be spending its Sunday afternoon there.
But then, on the way out with a Polish friend, we passed the new
concert hall. On an impulse, my friend persuaded the janitor to let
us slip in.

Darkness, devotion, opulent bass voices. Here, packed and
entranced, sat another and quite different Białystok listening to a
Russian choir singing Orthodox harmonies, a Białystok to whom
Solidarity's supreme festival of Polish patriotism and liberty a few
hundred yards away meant little. These were the Byelorussians,
and their dream was not the same.

In the town, beside the Solidarity posters, there were a few
small posters in Cyrillic script. I asked a Solidarity man who the
faces on them were. 'Oh, that's Sokrat Janowicz. He's a fanatical
Byelorussian nationalist—bilingual street-signs and all that.'

And this face?

'That's Gienek Mironowicz. Another Byelorussian activist, a
schoolmaster.'

In Warsaw, Lech Wałęsa and the main Citizens' Committee
(the name for Solidarity's campaign bureau) had pressed Solidarity
in Białystok to put Mironowicz on their regional candidates' list for
the Sejm. But the local Białystok Citizens' Committee had decided
against him. 'We reckoned that nobody would have heard of
him . . .'

After that conversation, I knew that I was going to have to
come back to Białystok. Elsewhere, Poland can seem almost
one-dimensional: anarchic in detail but uncannily uniform in
outline. Practically everyone speaks Polish with the same accent;
practically everyone is Catholic; practically everyone is anti-
communist and anti-Russian and quotes the same verses from the
same Romantic poets. But here, in the north-east, was a place
where I could stand and see Poland in a new way. Here at last were
the normal differences which most European countries contain—
differences of language and religion and political outlook. Here, I
thought, 'Polishness' would suddenly stand out in perspective, in
light and shade, in three dimensions.

When I returned, it was 13 August. In the frowsy heat wave, Białystok looked less like a city than a cluster of worn-out villages. The pink stucco railway station, blocked with queues waiting for tickets or newspapers or a bottle of mineral water, seemed too small for a place with 166,000 inhabitants. The taxi to the Hotel Cristal bolted along empty streets, past patches of waste land, wooden shacks, a few rows of petty shops. Where was this city, anyway? I remembered that the writer Maria Dąbrowska called this place 'shockingly ugly.' And that was in the 1930s, before it was twice captured by the German armies and once by the Red Army. In the final 'liberation', the Russians contrived to set the whole town centre alight while trying to bomb the railway station, which they missed. Most of the quarter down by the Biała stream had already been levelled by the Germans, who had used it as a ghetto until the time came to drive the Jews of Białystok to the gas chambers. I thought that I would do a couple of interviews and then get back as soon as decently possible to Warsaw.

Nobody has ever loved Białystok, and it shows. This was a textile city of little brick mills and plank-built sweat-shops. Białystok grew suddenly large and rich in the last century, when the Russian occupiers set up a customs border between the heartlands of the empire and what had been the old Kingdom of Poland. The cotton mills of Łódź in central Poland found themselves beyond the line, but Białystok was on the Russian side and its exports into the empire's endless market stayed duty-free.

On my first afternoon, I walked down Lipowa Street. The Queues were forming for meat, children's shoes, some rolls of cloth I couldn't see properly past the heads of shoppers. The kiosks had two notices glued up, written in ball-point. One said 'STRIKE ALERT'. The other said: 'BRAK . . .'—lack of: today, it was lack of cigarettes and matches.

Elderly men with noble faces cadged from one another without loss of dignity. Sir John Gielgud, wearing a brown suit and sandals, shuffled across the café to the Pope who—in a short-sleeved tartan shirt, sitting in front of a glass of beer—had just mashed out a Marlboro.

'Please, let the gentleman feel free to take two.'

Baltic Sea

Riga

LATVIA

LITHUANIA

Dvina

Gdansk

Vistula

Lipowy Most

Minsk

Białystok

Łódź

Warsaw

Brest

Byelorussia

Lublin

Pripyat

POLAND

Kiev

UKRAINE

Puzscza

Boundaries since 1945 (Yalta)

Boundaries in 1939

'I thank the gentleman graciously; he is too kind.'
Politically, Poland was being reborn. Economically, it was
dying day by day. A kilo of *polędwica* (sirloin) now cost one-sixth of
the average monthly wage. A taxi cost seventy-five per cent more
than it did five days before. A small cup of coffee in Warsaw's
Holiday Inn cost more than a first-class rail ticket to Białystok. And
there were no matches in Warsaw either.

But everywhere in Białystok the Solidarity election posters had
been reverently left on the walls to bleach away. I recognized them
from June: the Byelorussian ones, in contrast, had all been scraped
off. Next to the Catholic church on Lipowa, somebody had chalked:
'Communism to the junk-heap of history!' Somebody else had been
at work with a home-made stencil—a tank, a star and the words:
'Soviets Go Home.'

In New York, you can buy a pastry called a Bialy. It is softer and
chewier than a bagel, and it doesn't have a hole. This is about
the only tangible relic of one of the world's great Jewish cities;
there were times in the last century when most of Białystok's
inhabitants were Jews. Samuel Pisar, one of the very few of them to
have survived World War Two, lists in his book *Of Blood and Hope*
some of those who began life here: Ludwik Zamenhof, inventor of
Esperanto; Maxim Litvinov, Soviet commissar for foreign affairs;
General Yigal Yadin, Israeli chief of staff and the archaeologist of
Masada; Dr Albert Sabin who invented the oral polio vaccine. The
Jews, more than the Poles or the Byelorussians, were the real
founders of this city, the creators of its wealth and its culture, the
only people—perhaps—who did love it. To Samuel Pisar,
Białystok was 'once known as the Town with the Golden Heart.'
Nothing of that remains. A few buildings survive from the wartime
ghetto quarter, with a bust of Zamenhof and a street named after
Melmud, the hero who flung sulphuric acid at the SS during the final
ghetto rising. The Germans razed everything else. Where the
ghetto was, there is now an east-west bypass road, a strip of park, a
weedy sports ground. When I went there, they were digging a new
drain down by the Biała stream and, in the sand, lying exposed at
my feet, was the archaeology of the ghetto: foundations, glazed
tiles, fragments of china and glass. A rat, scrabbling to keep its

balance, was clambering over a mass of rusted bed-frame.

Back in the middle of town, I asked an old man where the synagogue had been. He pointed at an apartment block across the street.

It was there until that fire. It had a magnificent cupola. He used to pass it every day going to work. That was the Great Synagogue, and all the houses round here had been Jewish.

In those times, did he have Jewish friends?

'No, no,' he said, surprised. But then he went on: 'Of course, we were all at school together. There were so many Jewish boys in our class, so many . . .' Suddenly his face twisted and furrowed; he began to sob loudly. He said: 'I saw it—we couldn't help them—they were beyond help.' He turned away, choking on his tears. I put my arm round his shoulders, and we stood awkwardly together for a moment until he shuffled away. At first I thought that he was a bit deranged. But then it occurred to me that he had spoken those last few sentences not in Polish, but in a sort of German. Just possibly, he was himself Jewish.

I didn't follow him but walked across the street. On a tablet in the wall, it was written in Polish and Hebrew, that in this place, on 24 June 1941, the Germans burned 3,000 Jews who had been driven into the Great Synagogue. Two days after Hitler's invasion of the Soviet Union; two days after the Germans had captured the city for the second time.

From there, a taxi took me to the remaining Jewish cemetery on Wschodnia Street, on the outskirts (the old central cemetery has been bulldozed away to make a park). There was an iron Star of David on the gates, which were rusted open. Beyond them, I pushed my way into a dense little wood of thorny trees in which hundreds of tombs were sinking into the undergrowth. Many were broken, many looted for their marble slabs. Physically, I told myself, this was no worse than the condition of many Victorian Christian cemeteries in London. And yet the oblivion is infinitely deeper. Nobody comes or reads the Hebrew on the graves; nobody will ever come; there is nobody left. This stony thicket on Wschodnia Street now seems to have only one purpose these days: it provides a path—a short cut—to the Catholic cemetery next door. There, candles glow and families move busily among the graves.

51

That particular afternoon, the cemetery was busy: the Polish Catholics of Białystok were celebrating a big anniversary. The fifteenth of August is *Maria Wniebowzięcie*, the Assumption of the Virgin. But it is also the day of the Miracle on the Vistula. In 1920, the Bolshevik armies invaded newly independent Poland and at Białystok they installed a committee of Polish communists assigned to convert the nation into a Soviet republic. The Red Cavalry rode victoriously forward until it was approaching the suburbs of Warsaw. Then Józef Piłsudski, Poland's liberator and commander, mounted a counter-offensive that tore right across the Bolshevik rear, cutting off whole armies and severing their lines of communication. The Bolsheviks, whose advance patrols had been about to cross the German frontier into East Prussia, now fell back in disorder and were chased eastwards across Poland into the distant borderlands.

The Catholic families laying their flowers on the graves at Wschodnia Street told me that the big commemoration was on the other side of town, in the St Roch cemetery. At St Roch cemetery there was a wooden church, where I found crowds honouring the Virgin and the victory at once; a portrait of Piłsudski beside the altar and ribbons of the 1920 volunteers draped about.

With helpful gestures, the priest explained how Mary really was lifted up by the angels into the sky, just like in the pictures by Wit Stwosz and Murillo. He went on to imitate the Polish soldiers in 1920, who (he said) shouted, 'Long Live Maria! Let's die for her!' as they charged against the Bolshevik hordes. Poland, continued the priest, is the eastern bastion of Christendom. And that is why, he explained, the Polish soldier does not drink or steal or lie or kill anyone except his enemy. That is why every drop of blood shed by a Polish soldier is taken up to Heaven. That is also why every Polish soldier's suffering and torment is noted down by God. In 1920, 1939, 1944 'and afterwards' (he meant the savage partisan war against the communist regime that lasted for several years in the forest) the army of Poland has shed its blood so that we might live.

At the end, everyone sang 'The First Brigade', the marching song of Piłsudski's legions.

O n Sunday I went to a Russian Orthodox Mass. The church, on Lipowa Street, is in the town centre, a decorous Palladian building from the 1840s, where Czarist bureaucrats and Russian officers worshipped in the years when Białystok was a city of the empire. Now the worshippers are not the rulers but the underclass: the Byelorussian minority.

I was surprised to see so many young men in the congregation. The older generation tends to be squat and short-legged. But these were giants in T-shirts: they crossed themselves in the wide-sweeping, plucking Orthodox custom, and yet they looked out of place both among their parents and amid the conspicuous self-abasement of the ritual. Over and over again, the priest and the acolytes intoned the same solemn bass phrase; the worshippers drifted away into their own private raptures; the candles were raised and displayed and lowered again. Some men prostrated themselves. It was strange to attend, in Poland, a religious ceremony that seemed to have no nationalist emotion in it.

Or so I thought. Later I discovered that these same big, young men were the very representatives of nationalism: it was they who were the ones determined to graft Byelorussian politics into the Orthodox community. There may be shows of private rapture, but there was also public scheming. These young people were tired of their Church's passivity, exasperated that it clung to the Russian 'old Slav' language in the liturgy. They were pushing for the vernacular—Byelorussian, which is neither Polish nor Russian—to replace the Russian that was used in church. They were supported, I would also learn later, by the large emigrant Byelorussian communities in North America.

As things are, though, the Orthodox church in Poland feels like an outpost of Russian culture. This doesn't make it popular. And even before the war the Polish state encouraged Orthodoxy here for that very reason, calculating that its Russian flavour would alienate Byelorussian intellectuals, driving them gradually away from their own culture and towards integration into 'Polishness'. Since 1945, the new Communist regime in Poland has seemed at times to be protecting the Orthodox religion for the same devious reasons.

The last thing communist Poland or the Soviet Union wanted was an authentic Byelorussian revival. Phoney, controllable revivals, on the other hand, have frequently been useful. For many years the Byelorussians in Poland were restricted to a 'Social-Cultural Association' set up in the post-Stalin years under close supervision by the Ministry of the Interior. All attempts to set up genuine organizations for the Orthodox laity were squashed by the security police. The result was that a Byelorussian samizdat emerged alongside the enormous 'unofficial' literature of the Polish opposition, with periodicals like *Sustreci* and *Dakumenty*. This year, the Białystok authorities did finally agree that a lay Orthodox society called 'The Brotherhood' could be established. But their agreement amounts to too little, too late: 'The Brotherhood' is notably cautious and unpolitical and uses the Polish language, which isn't enough for the young militants of the Byelorussian cause. The attendance at Byelorussian cultural festivals and religious rallies this year was many times larger than it has ever been: a sign that the resistance of the Orthodox clergy and establishment to Byelorussian nationalism is going to break under pressure from below.

Across the frontier, the Byelorussian movement is moving more slowly. The Byelorussian grouping which calls itself 'Rebirth' is not as confident or militant as the National Fronts in the Baltic republics or as the 'Ryukh' movement in the Ukraine. Its programme so far is only to 'raise national consciousness' and to defend Byelorussian language and culture. But the authorities in Minsk, capital of Soviet Byelorussia and one of the last fortresses of unreconstructed Brezhnevism, refused for as long as they dared to let 'Rebirth' meet on their territory. Its founding congress had to be held at Vilnius, in Lithuania. Modest as it is, 'Rebirth' seems to have found the inevitable leader-icon which most nationalisms require: a young archaeologist Zenon Pozniak, described to me—without irony—by one Byelorussian as nothing less than the 'new Robespierre—an utterly true spirit.'

It wasn't until I was back in London that I read what Lech Wałęsa had written about all this, in the 'Letter to the Polish Electorate', published in April. He spoke of the national and religious minorities that still lived in Poland—calling them 'our rare and precious inheritance from the past'—and pointed out that 'they are concerned for the preservation, within the Polish environment, of their own religious and ethnic identity. They are concerned for their cultures, their schools, their churches. They want dignity, without having to 'change into Polish clothes.' Wałęsa insisted that the minorities should be involved in Solidarity's election campaign: that they should 'participate with the dignity to which they are entitled.'

There have been two competing ideologies in modern Polish nationalism. One is 'National Egoism', assuming an almost totalitarian priority for the interests of Poland at the expense of the interests of other nations. The doctrine implies that the true Poland is Catholic and Slav and that the other nationalities in the country—the Jews, above all, but also the Byelorussians, Ukrainians, Lithuanians and Germans—constitute a threat to Polish identity. The threat is both racial and political: these other peoples could not be expected to understand the absolute imperative of the Polish national struggle to regain the independence lost with the partitioning of the country in the eighteenth century. In the early years of this century, 'National Egoism' was the principle upheld by the politician Roman Dmowski, leader of the National Democrat movement (*Endecja* in Polish).

The other tradition is that of Józef Piłsudski, the man of the Miracle on the Vistula. The National Democrats and Roman Dmowski never managed to take power, but Piłsudski dominated independent Poland from 1918 to his death in 1935. Piłsudski, although authoritarian, believed in Poland as a multi-national federation. His dream was to revive the ancient Polish-Lithuanian Commonwealth, by recovering the eastern Borderlands which lay between Poland and Russia.

The Polish Commonwealth was an astonishing place. It matters now because of what is starting to happen in the territory between Poland and Russia. Before the Commonwealth was destroyed at the end of the eighteenth century, when Russia, Prussia and Austria partitioned the Polish state between them, it was, at its best, not only the biggest but the most tolerant state in northern Europe. It began from the medieval union of the Kingdom of Poland with the Grand Duchy of Lithuania. In the

Commonwealth, all subjects of the King and Grand Duke were 'Poles': Protestants and Jews as well as Catholics, Balts and Tartars, Scots and Byelorussians, as well as 'ethnic' Poles. It was a ramshackle structure whose tolerance at times broke down. It was, certainly, 'pre-modern'. But while it lasted the Commonwealth was one of Europe's nobler achievements.

Lech Wałęsa has made his own ideology clear. His nationalism, like that of the whole leading group in Solidarity, is Piłsudski's kind. But the nationalism of ordinary Poles, whether they are coal miners or peasants or petty officials, often has a lot of Roman Dmowski in its mix. Political anti-Semitism is common in its vulgar equation: Jew equals Red equals traitor to Polish independence. But the Slav minorities, the Byelorussians and Ukrainians who are mostly non-Catholic, are suspect too. These are the prejudices that arose from the Partitions and that continue today, reinforced by the practice of whatever regime is in power of divide-and-rule: bribing religious or national minorities in order to dissolve their alliance with the Polish-Catholic majority. As a result, the Ukrainians are accused by Poles of collaborating with Germans or Russians in order to further their own national cause, while the Byelorussians, almost all of them Orthodox in religion, have acquired a name for being ungrateful and untrustworthy.* After 1945 (this is what Poles in Białystok and the surrounding countryside constantly told me), the Byelorussians let themselves be used as the spoiled brats of the new communist regime. There were ushered into powerful jobs in the local Party and administration, while Orthodox applications to build churches got kinder treatment than those from Catholic parishes.

This isn't how the Byelorussians see it. Some 200,000 of them live in the Białystok region of Poland, a tiny overflow from the Soviet republic of Byelorussia with its nine million people. Their tradition has been to keep their heads down, a lesson learned from

---

* Since last summer, the opening of the Soviet frontier allowed Polish visitors to discover more about the genocidal massacres of the Polish minority committed by Ukrainians during the three years of Nazi occupation. In the region of Volhynia, for instance, whole villages were destroyed and all the inhabitants killed.

two centuries of intermittent Russian tyranny. But there was a time when Byelorussians were assertive and proud.

On my first night in Białystok, I went to see the Byelorussian intellectual Sokrat Janowicz in his small flat near the town centre. He told me that the Grand Duchy itself had once been Byelorussian in race and language. Lithuanian? In those days, Janowicz said, the word meant Byelorussian. The people who now call themselves Lithuanians, he assured me, were a backward Baltic race who in those days lived in the swamps of Żmudź. It was only after the fall of the Grand Duchy that the nature of the Byelorussians began to change, transforming them into the most humble and least assertive of all the peoples of the Borderlands. They became—and Janowicz quoted the passage cited at the beginning of this piece—the people whom Konwicki thought 'too good and gentle and generous' for this world.

Until last summer. Then, in the Poland of Solidarity's triumph, Byelorussians began to raise their heads. Byelorussian nationalists campaigned openly and dared to use their own language on public election platforms. But all the suspicions of recent history revived as well.

Today Solidarity and the new Byelorussian movement seem to agree on only one point: that the communist system has been a calamity. Beyond that, though, they don't know what to make of one another.

A fter the Orthodox Mass, I walked across the city to Bem Street. I had heard something about its open-air market; this was the place to see Soviet Byelorussians, who were pouring across the frontier in order to trade. Once the old town of Grodno on the river Niemen had been the natural capital of the whole region, but in 1945 it had vanished behind the new Soviet border. Now, Soviet Byelorussia was coming across into Poland, making Białystok its market-place.

If there's nothing to buy in Soviet shops, it must be because it's being sold on Bem Street. Hundreds of cars with Soviet plates were drawn up round the market field. Whole families had spread out their goods on folding tables, on car bonnets, on gaudy scarves laid across the mud, and they were selling things they had bought 'over there', or inherited, or made, or simply stolen from their work-places. Polish buyers—from Warsaw or even further—come to Bem Street for bargains.

This trade, though done with money, was really an exchange of manufactured goods for food. It may seem incredible that anyone should travel to Poland in order to buy food. But conditions in the western Soviet Union are so bad that they make even Poland look abundant. For Polish zloties, the Soviet Byelorussians were selling car parts, rugs, cosmetics, Indian toothpaste, Aeroflot cigarettes, pencil sharpeners like miniature lathes, lavatory pans, caviar, Turkish sweaters, computer games in Cyrillic, packets of Georgian tea, knickers and bras made in the Ukraine, hairdryers, electric samovars . . . Soviet television sets, half the price of Polish ones, were now a banned export. Instead, there was an inrush of the ugliest toys in the world: purple Lunakhod moon-buggies, four different sorts of battery-driven tank with red star and working missiles, glumpish dolls, clockwork bears which shake their heads slowly from side to side and groan.

At one side of the field, among the sausage-stalls, women were selling gold, whispering in bad Polish to their customers. Men wandered through the crowd with notices hung round their necks: 'I buy dollars, marks, forints, crowns.' Some even bought roubles at the discounted Polish price. Eventually all the devalued zloties earned on Bem Street would be spent in the food shops or even at the back door of meat-processing plants. There was a nasty fight this June at the town of Ełk, when the regular black-market purchasers from Grodno turned up at the canned-meat plant with an articulated truck and found that a strike was going on. Everywhere in the region, somebody knows somebody who actually saw the back of a Soviet lorry burst open and release an avalanche of loaves and rolls over the highway.

Once, Białystok had an Orthodox church, a Catholic church and a Great Synagogue, all about the same size. But between the wars, after Poland had regained its independence, the Catholic Poles began to erect the St Roch Basilica, a monster of concrete fretwork and lattice blocking one end of Lipowa Street. After 1945 there was an Orthodox counter-offensive. It started with a crop of onion domes in the villages of the region and culminated in a cathedral that was completed this year in the Antoniuk suburb of Białystok. Then came Solidarity. Opposite the Orthodox cathedral in Antoniuk, a new Catholic church, the size of an airship hangar, was slowly crawling up its wooden scaffolding. Near the towers of the Sloneczny Stok housing scheme, the foundation for yet another church had appeared.

You could argue that, in a country with a shortage of building materials, where the waiting time for a flat can be thirty years, this was a queer way to use its resources. But nobody would listen to you. The rattle of Orthodox and Catholic collection-boxes was loud and urgent. Much of the Orthodox building programme was being paid for by the Byelorussian emigrants in Canada and the United States, which was why—in the end—the Byelorussian language would get into those churches whatever the misgivings of the priesthood. As for the Polish Catholics, the building of a church still amounted to the raising of one more tower on that 'bastion against the East'. Especially in Białystok.

The day before I left, I went out to a block of flats at Sloneczny Stok, on a windy slope south of the city. The tower-block was new, but already decayed. Here lived a man and his daughter who, I had been told, would give me a insight into the spirit of Solidarity in Białystok. The father was an old man He produced a photograph of his own father as the only Polish clerk in a Czarist Russian bank in Białystok. The old man himself had been in a Soviet prison, in the Home Army resistance against the Nazi occupation, in three concentration camps (Gross-Rosen, Nordhausen, Bergen-Belsen). He said to me: 'Poland is fulfilling its mission. In 1920 we saved Europe from Bolshevism. So now Poland has begun the destruction of communism all over the world, even in Russia. Only Solidarity made Gorbachev possible, and only Solidarity could show the way ahead to national movements everywhere . . .'

His daughter Zosia came in from Mass. She was a member of the regional executive of Solidarity: the trade union, that is, not the Citizens' Committee wing that had organized the election

59

campaign. She worked underground with the union throughout the years of martial law after 1981, when it was banned, but she escaped arrest.

I had met Polish women of Zosia's kind before. She was beautiful, utterly sure of herself and of the righteousness of her cause, a severe moralist. Women who fought in the Warsaw Rising of 1944 are often like her, still measuring their own behaviour and that of others by the purity and devotion of those sixty-three days. To behave loosely or basely is to betray the sacrifice. Virtue is the true patriotism.

We talked about who was supposed to control the new Solidarity parliamentarians: the senators and deputies in the Sejm. I couldn't work out to whom they were democratically accountable: was it to Solidarity, or to their electors or to the Citizens' Committees which selected them as candidates in the first place?

Zosia simply didn't see a problem. It had to be Solidarity. Why should there be a separate political party in addition to the union? 'In the Citizens' Committee here, there is an ambitious group, but I say that, ethically and morally, the group is not entitled to be in the position to govern. We, in the union, on the other hand, we have passed the eight-year test of clandestinity; we were persecuted and lost our jobs. It is we who have the moral right to instruct the parliamentarians. And if they need an annual conference on policy, then they can attend the congress of Solidarność—the union's own congress—alongside the ordinary delegates from the factories. Solidarity is universal.'

I asked her about Byelorussian candidates in the June elections. Was it true that Lech Wałęsa had urged the Citizens' Committee here to run an Orthodox candidate for the Sejm and had suggested the schoolteacher Eugeniusz Mironowicz? Had there been a hope that, in such a case, the Orthodox bishop might instruct his flock to vote for Solidarity? And why did the Białystok Citizens' Committee decide against Mironowicz *and* against the idea of running Sokrat Janowicz, the Byelorussian writer, as a candidate for the Senate? Was the Citizens' Committee's membership exclusively Polish-Catholic?

Zosia replied that, when the next elections were fought, she would want to see a candidate from the ethnic minority on the

Solidarity list. She knew Mironowicz and his brother well; she had taught them both history. But she complained that the Byelorussians did not yet have a coherent or united attitude to Solidarity. 'Yes, we were asked if we would adopt Sokrat Janowicz for the Senate. But he wrote a poem attacking the Pope. It was impossible!'

Her father, listening closely, broke in. 'We had Orthodox boys as well as Catholics with us in the Home Army. And they fought and died for Poland at Monte Cassino too . . . '

Listening to father and daughter, I saw that there was no way to fit their view of what had happened to that of the Byelorussian politicians. I had already been to see both the men she had mentioned: Janowicz, on my first evening, and Mironowicz in his comfortable wooden house in the outskirts, where the streets become sand-tracks and run into the fields. Both insisted that they had never had any intention of joining the Solidarity platform, although both were invited to do so. And both of them swore to me that as Byelorussians they would have been committing political suicide by associating with Solidarity.

In the end, they had run as independent Byelorussian candidates for Senate and Sejm. They lost. But they scored impressively in some of the Orthodox villages, where Solidarity did very badly.

Mironowicz turned out to be precisely one of those tall young men I had seen in church, with a rich moustache. Sokrat Janowicz, an older man with many books to his name, is a dark, square-set man with a bad leg. Janowicz told me: 'The Byelorussian people are afraid of Solidarity. They think it represents the recidivist Catholic fanaticism of old Poland, and if the Byelorussians thought I was with Solidarity, I would be finished.' In fact, exactly that rumour had been put about. The Orthodox church, still nervous of the Byelorussian nationalist revival and frightened of Polish reprisals, spread the rumour that Janowicz was 'crypto-Solidarity' and backed its own candidate against him (who campaigned exclusively in the Polish language). The Communists, sly to the last, also warned the Orthodox community that Janowicz was a Solidarity man. Solidarity, in return, contrived to imply that Janowicz was actually a Communist puppet wearing Byelorussian folk-costume.

61

It was a mess. But next time, the two men say, it will be better. A Byelorussian Citizens' Committee is soon to be set up, the nucleus of a political party which will contest the local elections. At this stage, the aims will be modest: 'cultural autonomy', their own language in the schools, bilingual road signs, a say in regional planning to halt the drain of population from the villages.

But 4 June—election day—was none the less a turning-point for the Byelorussians in Poland. As soon as Sokrat Janowicz began to speak in Byelorussian from a platform, a dead hush fell. 'I felt my own rashness, breaching this moral complex, using a tongue until now spoken only at home or among friends, or maybe at functions with invited guests, but never at a public rally. I was warned by other Byelorussians not to dare, because there was sure to be some Polish chauvinist around who would start throwing stones.'

Are matters that bad? Sokrat Janowicz rages against 'Poles who are ill with an anti-Russian complex, and a Catholicism sick with colonialism. Poland and Russia have the same imperial complexes, the one about empire lost, the other about empire won . . .' But he admits that 'we have no problem with the younger Polish generation.'

I asked Janowicz who now had the effective power in Białystok.

He shrugged. The Communist authorities, he said, were still going to their offices. Local government remained for the moment in their hands, and the First Secretary of the Party in Białystok was still a personage. But now, as that dustbin of history opened for them, Janowicz reported that the Communists had changed tactic. After decades of playing the Orthodox community off against the Catholics without giving much to either, the Communists were spending their last months granting all the Byelorussian demands that they used to reject: access to local radio, teaching in Byelorussian, special grants to farmers in Orthodox districts.

Perhaps, as Janowicz thought, it was because they had lost their sense of power. Perhaps, though, this was only another hand in the divide-and-rule game, one more shuffle and deal of that greasy old minority card—this time, against Solidarity.

History will label 1989 as the Third Springtime of Nations. There was 1848 and then 1918: the dream of escape from empires, and then the awakening as the empires collapsed. Now comes 1989, in which every nation between the Elbe and the Pacific is simmering: 'historic' nations like the Magyars, Serbs and Georgians, suppressed nations like the Lithuanians, Byelorussians and Meshketians, recently-invented nations like the Azeris or the Macedonians. But the reviving of nations is not the raising of a Lazarus from the dead. The problem is that under one Lazarus there generally lies another. Poland rises joyfully from the grave, disclosing buried national minorities which in turn wriggle to be resurrected.

The Annus Mirabilis is breeding national movements and revivals throughout the swathe of territory which separates Poland from the heartlands of Russia: in Lithuania and the other Baltic nations, in Soviet Byelorussia, in the Ukraine. At the same time, the present Soviet frontier which divides those people from their kin within Poland has suddenly turned porous.

In the age of the Commonwealth, it was Poland rather than Russia which was the imperial power in these borderlands. There are still many Polish patriots who assume that, once Russian power fails, the smaller nations in between will gladly return to Polish protection.

But this is wrong. None of these national movements, from Sajudis in Lithuania to Ryukh in the Ukraine, wants to exchange Moscow for Warsaw. The future depends, first, upon what happens to Mikhail Gorbachev. But after that, if there is to be any kind of distinct future for the borderlands, everything will depend on the form which Polish nationalism takes.

Tom Nairn, in *The Breakup of Britain*, made popular the idea of nationalism as a Janus: one face turned to the future, another backwards towards the past. The dualism in Solidarity is about the two Janus-faces of Polish nationalism, the most striking of all examples to support Nairn's argument. It is exactly the backward-looking face of Polish patriotism which bears the features we would now call 'progressive' or 'enlightened'. The Wałęsa leadership looks back to the Commonwealth (naturally through a golden haze) for holy notions like tolerance and the ideal of multi-racialism. The nationalism of Roman Dmowski and the *Endecja*—in its way 'modern' if compared to the revivalism of a pre-modern past— taught the then-fashionable doctrines of state-worship, the mass party, national egoism and racial destiny. But those values, in contrast, have long since been discarded along with the rest of Europe's reactionary rubbish.

It comes hard to most Poles to accept that Poland could be perceived by weaker nations as an oppressor, aggressor or imperial power. That doesn't fit the image of Messianism: of Poland-as-immaculate-victim, of the curriculum which presents Poland as Europe's martyr and redeemer. In Białystok, Polish faces would change from bewilderment to outrage when I quoted Sokrat Janowicz's remarks about what Byelorussian voters thought of Solidarity. But that self-obsession, that lack of the capacity to think oneself into another's skin, has to break down if there is to be safety in Eastern Europe.

For the moment, Poland is in the right hands. Tadeusz Mazowiecki and his cabinet belong to the sort of Polish patriot who fought all over nineteenth-century Europe 'for your freedom and ours'. The new government in Warsaw represents that young element in Solidarity which cleans up Jewish graveyards and campaigns for the re-opening of Ukrainian churches. Yet Poland is once again on the way to becoming a power in east-central Europe. Nationalism is breaking loose in the old lands of the Grand Duchy, as Russian control slackens. Nobody yet knows what might replace the Soviet imperium in the borderlands—a new alliance, or supra-national trading bloc, a political federation?—but whatever grows up through the threadbare remains of the Warsaw Pact and Comecon, Poland will have the capacity to dominate it. The way Poland behaves in the next couple of years towards its own national minorities—difficult and elusive groups, who often don't clearly know what they want—will tell the rest of the world something about how the Poles will use that power.

MICHAEL IGNATIEFF
TURIA

1 November 1983

Turia's room is at the end of an aquamarine-tiled corridor in a mansion in Holland Park, built for a department-store millionaire before the First War and now used as a half-way house for mental patients. She is one of their house mothers.

'I love my lunatics,' she says.

The 'lunatics' are away for the weekend. We are alone in the house. Her room is small, painted a faded yellow. There is a table crowded with violets in little pots in front of a window that looks out over the garden, and around the table a pile of old plastic bags filled with biscuits and letters, cosmetics and old bills. Her dressing-table is strewn with eye-liner, mascara, cleansers, creams, face-powder and talcum. On the bedside table, a large radio from Boots, some tapes of the Bulgarian tenor Boris Christof and some devotional books by Metropolitan Anthony Bloom of the Russian Orthodox Church as well as a large colour photograph of him with full beard and sacerdotal robes.

It is dark. The curtains are drawn and the room is small and close. She is propped up on cushions on her bed. Her hair is pulled up on top of her head, like a Gibson girl in an Edwardian theatrical advertisement, and held in place by a hair-net decorated with a bright red bow. Her eyelids are painted eggshell blue. She is small and delicate, fine-boned, wearing black linen trousers and a white ruffled blouse. She has little black patent leather pumps on her feet. There is one large ring with a cameo portrait of the Emperor Paul on it, which she rotates around her finger as she speaks. Her hands are thin, black-veined, her bones wrapped in translucent, liver-spotted skin. She is eighty-six years old.

'So we are in our sitting-room, on either side of the fire, the Grand Duchess and I, and we are doing our needle-point. It is evening, and everything is quiet. Suddenly, the shutters are being shaken, the servants are crying out, someone is shouting that the gates must be opened this instant. The door bursts open at the end of the room and there are a dozen men in black coats brandishing revolvers. My needle-point drops into my lap. I am staring. They are staring. But the Grand Duchess does not drop a stitch. So that they can hear, she says, *"Ma chère, vous négligez votre travail."*'

I say: 'This must be in September 1918.'
'I don't remember. In Kislovodsk anyway.'
I say: 'They arrested my grandfather the same night.'
'And do you know the miraculous thing? The savages never came a step closer. It was as if there was an invisible circle around us, beyond which they would not dare to step. They just stood there in the door, their mouths open, watching us and our needle-point.'

Next day, she took a train to Pyatigorsk Party headquarters and demanded the return of the Grand Duchess's silver.

'But you were crazy!' I say.

'I was twenty years old, darling.'

She was shown into the commissar's office.

' "Shake my hand," he says. I will not. "Then," he says, "I will kill you." He is playing with the pistol. I think: Will I hear the shot or will I be dead already? A moment passes.'

She pushes a cigarette into the holder, lights it with a flick of her lighter and blows smoke high into the air. She holds the holder in the old way, from the underside, between thumb and forefinger.

'Then, my dear, it ceased being what it was and became just a man facing a woman. I could see he thought I was attractive and, when I saw that, I knew I was safe.'

I look around the room. On a dresser there is a photograph of two American grandchildren and a picture of her with her brother, Lapin, who went to Chicago and became a businessman. I ask whether she has a photograph of her husband. She shakes her head.

'Why should he be imprisoned so—in one pose—when there were all those days still remaining to me?'

She looks me over. 'Why have you come to see me? We are cousins, of course, *mais il faut pas exagérer.*'

'Father said, "If you want to know what my mother was really like, you must visit Turia." '

She laughs, looking at me with wry disbelief. 'Me? Your grandmother? Darling, you must be joking!'

1 March 1984

It is a bright, blustery day. Downstairs, under the blue Byzantine mosaic in the hallway, the patients are reading the newspapers. A girl is staring into deep space. A boy with a beard is saying something I do not catch. She meets me in the hallway, leaning on a black and silver cane, nods to 'her lunatics' and very slowly ascends the stairs. When I ask her what she has been up to, she says, as she pegs along the blue-tiled corridor: 'I have been praying for Monsieur Andropov. Poor man, someone must pray for him.'

'But he was KGB.'

'Then he needs all the prayers he can get.'

She makes the tea, heating the water with the little coil immersion on top of her dresser. One tea-bag per cup. Plop. Plop. Her hands shake. The tea spatters when she passes it to me.

'How are you?'

'Awful. I am in my coffin already, just waiting for someone to screw down the lid.'

She smiles and lowers herself on to the bed, slowly pulls her legs up and lies back with a sigh of exhaustion. '*Alors, jeune homme, raconte.*'

I take out the little photo of four children, in sailor's suits, shielding their eyes from the sun, standing on a gravel pathway in front of a great house, in front of a man with mutton-chopped whiskers and an apron around his waist.

'One of them is you.'

'Where did you get this?'

'Grandmother's photo album of Doughino.' Turia is the last person alive to have seen the English garden, the greenhouses, the little children's theatre under the eaves, and the great library with Panin's statue at the end by the French windows. All I have are the photographs.

She uses her glasses as a lorgnette, holding them between thumb and forefinger and staring close and long at the little photo. She shakes her head.

I prompt: 'The prettiest one, there on the end.'

'Could be,' she says, handing back the photo. And then, quite sharply, 'Prettiest one? You are joking. In all pictures that I remember there are three beauties—Aga, Fuga, Alecka—and one little pig, with three chins and hairs sticking out of the top of its head. That was me.'

I won't buy this. No, no. 'My Uncle Dima remembers on a

summer holiday at Vybiti, 1915, crawling through the high grass by the river-bank with his brothers and watching you, Aga and Fuga bathing naked on the other bank.'

'I hope it was a rewarding sight.'

'You were the most rewarding sight of all.'

'Who am I to contradict your Uncle Dima?'

Long pause. She lights a cigarette, sucks it right down into her lungs.

'I do remember when I first felt I was a woman, when I felt the power I had. It was at the ball in Petrograd with my cousin in his uniform from the Corps de Pages. Very elegant, my dear. There was this waltz, where your hands hardly touched, but everything below the waist was positively *welded* together. As he whirled me around, I could feel his pleasure in dancing with me. I knew I could do anything with him that I wanted.'

She exhales deeply. Her eyes narrow and she thinks. 'I was a success with men—this is hard to put into words—but I did not abuse my power.'

More thought, a longer pause. She looks out over the lawn, at the naked trees shivering in the wind.

She looks at me. 'I wonder about you. Are you very interested in sex?'

She is eighty-seven years old and the fire of her attraction is far from out: the little red bows in her hair, the faultless crease in her black linen trousers, the way she touches your hand when you light her cigarette. But I choose to say: 'Ask my wife.'

They met once and Turia said to her, wagging her finger: 'My dear, if I was twenty years younger, I would make you worry about these little afternoons I spend with your husband.'

15 July 1984

We are in the garden, on lawn chairs, underneath her window. She is wearing a print dress and her nails are painted bright red. She has on a raffish pair of Ray Ban sunglasses.

'My cousin married an officer in the Hussars, handsomest fellow in creation. Murdered by his men in the revolution. For years she slept with his blood-stained tunic on the pillow beside her.'

'Turia! How am I supposed to believe that?'
'I swear it. Then she married a Kleinmichel, ugliest person you ever saw, who kept his false teeth in one pocket and his hearing-aid in the other.'
'Turia!'
'I swear it!'

4 September 1984

Someone in the house has stolen her signet ring, the large one with the tiny enamel portrait of the Emperor Paul.
'I know who did it, poor darling. He brings me coffee in the morning. I cannot bear to look at him.'
'But you must do something.'
She shrugs. 'I have no proof. I just know.' She is not as dejected as I expect. I ask why. She tells me a story.

Her sister married a Hungarian, who left her when the Red Army moved into Budapest in 1945. Everyone was at the end of their tether. Her little apartment was requisitioned by the Soviets as a billet for officers. One of these officers and his blond mistress stole all her jewellery, the last remains of what she had brought out after the revolution. This pair had been stealing their way westwards into Europe, and the Soviet military police caught up with them in her sister's apartment.

'So these Soviet policemen spread the jewellery out on her kitchen table, not just hers, but everything that had been stolen right across Europe, and they say to my sister, identify just one piece as yours and we will take these two out into the courtyard and shoot them this minute.'

Turia plays with her wedding band, rotating it around her knuckle.

'My sister thought: I am tired of all this killing. So she looked at her jewellery, spread out on the table and said she didn't recognize any of it. The policeman wrapped her things up in a table-cloth and took the culprits away.'

'And what happened then?'

She looks at me. 'It made no difference. They were shot in the next town anyway.'

12 April 1985

'My legs, darling, someone seems to have borrowed them. We simply must have a taxi.' I hail one, lift her in. Her arms are painfully thin. We are going to the Good Friday service. She is dressed in black, no make-up, her face paper-white. She stares out at the rain-smeared London streets.

'What are you thinking?'

'My father wanted to be a monk. A devout, retiring man. Every Good Friday service in our chapel at Marino, he would assist our priest and the deacons carrying the icon from the sanctuary to the centre of the church. Carrying out the body of Christ, it is called. I remember his face.'

I find her a chair by a pillar and stand at the back, leaving her alone, keeping my distance. The choir sings softly while Metropolitan Anthony intones the prayers:

Like a thief I will acknowledge thee.
Remember me, O Lord, in thy kingdom.

She holds an unlit candle in her hand. The procession begins its passage from the altar to the centre of the church. The stiff black vestments of the clergy creak and sway. The icon is borne before them. They are carrying out the body of Christ. Turia is in profile by the pillar, wiping the tears from her cheeks with the back of her hand.

2 October 1985

Pneumonia. On her return from Chicago she was in a coma for ten days. She is lying in hospital propped up on her pillows. I have never seen her hair down before, loose around her shoulders. She manages a little wave and sinks back, gasping and rasping.

Alecka, her sister, is there from Chicago, pacing up and down in the hall outside, smoking furiously. She looks about seventy and is in fact eighty-five. Her voice blends Chicago with Saint Petersburg. 'She was very close. I was just going out for cigarettes and the nurse said, "I wouldn't, not just yet. It could happen any moment." '

I return to her bedside. The flowers are banked in rows on shelves. I take her hand, a little envelope full of bones, the untended nails yellow and claw-like. Her pulse flutters under my thumb like a little bird's.

19 November 1985

She is propped up, and they have combed her hair. I feed her a biscuit. She laughs weakly. 'The lady from the hospital library came round today. I said I'll have something light. She handed me a Barbara Cartland. "Just the thing, Mrs Campbell." Not for me, dear, I may be falling to pieces but I'm not yet ready for Barbara Cartland.'

25 November 1985

An old suitor, former colleague in the BBC, appears in the doorway, with a box of chocolates in his hands as small as he is large. He grins, 'Here I am, the unrequited lover.'
'You certainly are faithful. I will give you that.'
'Never answered my phone calls.'
'That is a considerable exaggeration.'
'Always in someone else's bed.'
'Don't be vulgar.'
They beam at each other. I leave them to it.

24 December 1985

She is spending Christmas in the hospital, at the invitation of the nurses, two of whom have volunteered to come in and keep her entertained.

She nibbles her biscuit and whispers, 'They are scheming behind my back to send me to Chicago to live with my son. Dear God! I love my son but I hate America!'

She settles into a story, which she punctuates with waves of the biscuit.

'After mother and Lapin got out of prison in Russia, they came to London—it was 1924—for an interview with an American businessman, the president of Edison Power of Chicago, at a suite in the Hyde Park Hotel. Mother's English was very bad, and Lapin's was worse, and so I came from Paris to help them out. I remember I wore a simple little suit and a black hat out to here. Very chic.

'Anyway, my mother is wearing her widow's weeds, a black coat to the floor, which from age and poverty and imprisonment had turned brown. She is carrying a bag containing her Russian Bible and her knitting. And Lapin is wearing the only suit he could afford, and the three of us are sitting in the lobby of the Hyde Park Hotel. My dear, we sat there for three hours. Three times, they call us up, three times, they say the great man is not ready. Three times, my mother takes out her Bible and her knitting.

'Finally, we are all ushered into his penthouse suite. Immediately the president of Edison Power begins abusing my poor brother in the foulest language imaginable. You so and so, what makes you think I am going to give a good-for-nothing like you a job? I sold newspapers on the Loop when I was twelve and so on. And my brother is smiling and thinking he is being complimented in some strange American way, and my mother is sitting there with her Bible and her knitting, tears streaming down her face.

'Finally I said, "That's enough. I am tired of your vulgarity. This boy worked day and night to get his mother out of prison and to keep the family alive after the revolution. He is what he is. It is not his fault."

'The American looks me up and down in my Paris suit. "That's the way to talk to me. I like your spirit. I'll give him the job, but that's the last favour I'll ever do for him. Now get out."'

She shrugs. 'So that is America.'

24 April 1986

She prevails. She does not go to America. But the half-way house decides she is too old to stay, especially at the weekends when she is alone. Alecka and her son find her a nursing home in Pimlico. Her suitcases are packed. The plastic bags full of biscuits and cosmetics and letters are piled up against the wall. She surveys the tiny accumulation of her life.

'Look what I've found among the debris,' she says.

Pictures of Marino: the stone lions on either side of the entrance, the servants massed on the steps; the sitting-rooms with the floor-to-ceiling Dutch stoves and the Chinoiserie silk wallpaper. Some of the sofa cushions bear the weight of recently departed bodies. Room after room is bare. In the greenhouse there are spider ferns and a full plaster cast of the Apollo Belvedere.

'There were a hundred rooms, and most of them had no heating. We went there in 1905, after the revolution. I remember eating my dinner with napkins wrapped around the silver because it was too cold to the touch.'

She hands me the packet of photographs, agrees with a shrug when I ask to copy them, indifferent to them, as if nothing could compare to the precision and detail of memory.

I wonder constantly how she makes a unity of so much time. She remembers hearing news of the Russo-Japanese War at the breakfast table at Marino! She nursed soldiers during the First War and broadcast on the BBC in the Second. She has lived to see Gorbachev. It seems that she can make sense of all this time only if her memory remains stuck in a groove, only if the past remains the same, frozen in the telling. I wonder whether she still recalls new things from her childhood. She thinks I have asked a very odd question indeed.

'Of course, darling. Heavens yes! This morning, sitting among my boxes and suitcases, this scene at Marino came into my mind when I was about eight and the Archbishop of Novgorod came to visit. He got out of his carriage and I thought: "Where is his luggage?" He had none. He came for one night and liked it so much he stayed with us for three weeks. Still no luggage. The state of his linen, dear, doesn't bear thinking about.'

Christmas 1986

I phone her to say I can't come in because I've slipped a disc. She clicks her tongue and says, 'Men are so hopeless, always pretending that they can cope, pretending the pain is not there. Women know the pain is there. They never pretend. What a silly boy you are.'

'Thanks a lot,' I say from my bed. 'And how are you?'

'Very low. First Christmas without a single member of my

family around. But I have had a talk with myself.'

19 January 1987

We are talking about fat men. She says, 'Life is very unfair. I've known men who were attracted to fat women, but I've never known a woman attracted to a fat man.'
I object.
She is formal. 'No, no, it is chemically impossible.'

12 April 1987

'I go to the bank. I ask for Mr Brazier. No one knows who I am talking about. Awful. Then I remember Mr Brazier is in the Pall Mall branch. All the way home in the taxi, I am sobbing. Dearest, you can get used to walking with a stick, but really to forget something like that, it is the beginning of the end.

'I feel like a boiled fish. Really, it is too boring. I can't wait to die. It will be such an adventure.'

She insists on accompanying me to the door. I ask if we couldn't do without this ritual, but she is stern. 'Absolutely not. We are not savages, after all.' And I lift her up and hand her the cane and hold the doors and she pads very, very slowly down the corridor, past the open doors, where the old ladies are babbling in front of the television sets.

We kiss each other on the cheek, three times. I bend almost double to reach her. She holds on to me for a minute.

'What is it about we Russians and goodbyes? Everyone else is so much more sensible. I see the English at airports, you know, a peck on the cheek, utterly dry-eyed, while us, my dear, clutching each other as if we were about to drown. That is why we age so badly—we've used all our emotions already.'

Then she is gone, padding slowly back down the corridor to her room, past the open door where an old woman is crying for her mother to come, over and over again.

8 November 1987

Pneumonia again. Metropolitan Anthony came to say prayers at her bedside. I expect the worst, but when I arrive she is propped up in bed eating an egg sandwich. I can't believe it. Her oldest friend, Rosemary, is there—winks at me—and resumes the task of getting her to sign the cheques on her pension book so Rosemary can draw her out the money.

Laboriously Turia makes faint pencil crosses on the signature line. She sinks back, and Rosemary removes the egg sandwich from her hand.

The heavy brocade curtains have been drawn. The room is smaller than ever, the light heavy and smudged. We both sit by her bedside. I hold her hand, purple and cold. Her eyes are shut, but she rubs her thumb against mine, a steady movement like the pulse, as if drawing the heat from my hand into hers. Her veins are dark, the skin translucent like rice-paper. All of her concentration is on her breathing: hoarse, shallow but determined.

She opens her eyes after a while and says, faintly, 'We must resume our discussions,' and then slips away again.

15 December 1987

Next to her on the hospital ward, there is a huge man naked from the waist, in a leg cast, watching daytime TV; on the other side, a man in striped blue jockey shorts, reading an Arthur Hailey novel and irritably scratching his crotch. Across the way, an old man is staggering to his feet and undoing his dressing-gown.

I say: 'I've got to get you out of here.'

'Indeed you do. The doctors tell you nothing and when they do, they make you feel they are doing you a tremendous favour.'

Her wrists are badly swollen. She is not eating. There is something feverish and exalted about her mood.

'The old man opposite, look at him, poor thing, he can barely walk. Now look at him, he is coming to give me a lecture. He has taken off his dressing-gown.'

I turn. He is indeed coming towards us in his underwear.

'This is not very promising. If he thinks we are going to make love, he is very much mistaken.'

77

15 May 1988

She is back in the nursing home, lying on her side, and I see the bare bones of her chest, the hip joints exposed beneath her night-gown. Her forehead is larger, rounder, the hollows around and under her eyes are deeper, the veins in her arms, black. Metropolitan Anthony had been there in the morning, to pray with her. His portrait is by her side.

Her questions have lost their focus. To catch anything at all, she must cast the net very wide: 'How old are your children?'

I have told her many times. She drifts asleep. Ten minutes later, she wakes, looks at me and says: 'Are you a success?'

12 June 1988

I tell her, holding her hand, feeling the pulse beating very faintly beneath the purplish cold skin, that I want to write the story of her life.

'Foolish idea. All lies.'

I say, no, no, it would be a novel.

She smiles, very faintly, eyes shut: 'More lies.'

15 July 1988

She is getting smaller and smaller. Just like a little girl.

Scraped to the bone. I hold her hand. My face is next to hers. I can barely make out what she says: 'Now we will have to do without our privileges. Now we have to go on alone.'

8 September 1988

Her coffin is in the centre of the Russian Church in Ennismore Gardens. Everyone who ever knew her—from all the corners and compartments of her life, old boy-friends, old colleagues, old confidants, young admirers, ancient Russians—are there. Her sister Alecka stands in the front, straight-backed and regal side by side Turia's son. We are holding lighted candles. Wax drips on to our hands. The choir is singing 'Eternal memory' and Metropolitan Anthony stands beside the coffin in his vestments, watching our tears fall.

PATRICK ZACHMANN
THE DEATH
OF MERAB KOSTAVA

Independence demonstration, Tbilisi, Georgia, 11 October 1989.

Funeral service for Merab Kostava in Zioni Cathedral, Tbilisi.

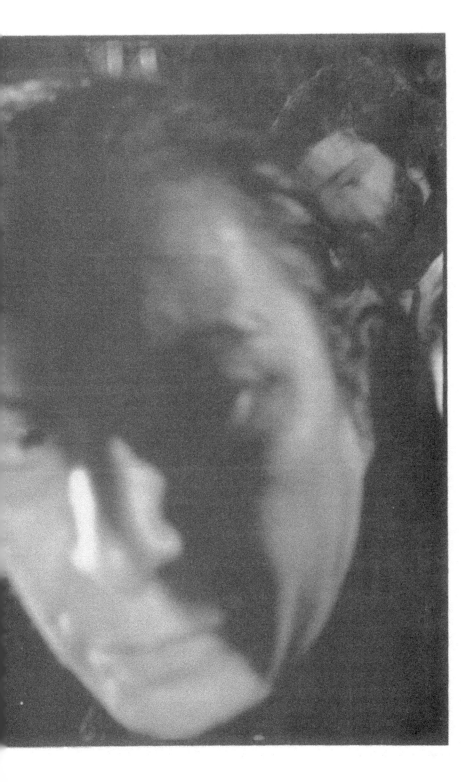

A couple next to a picture of their daughter killed in the April massacre .

Young Georgian girl watching black-market video of 5 April massacre.

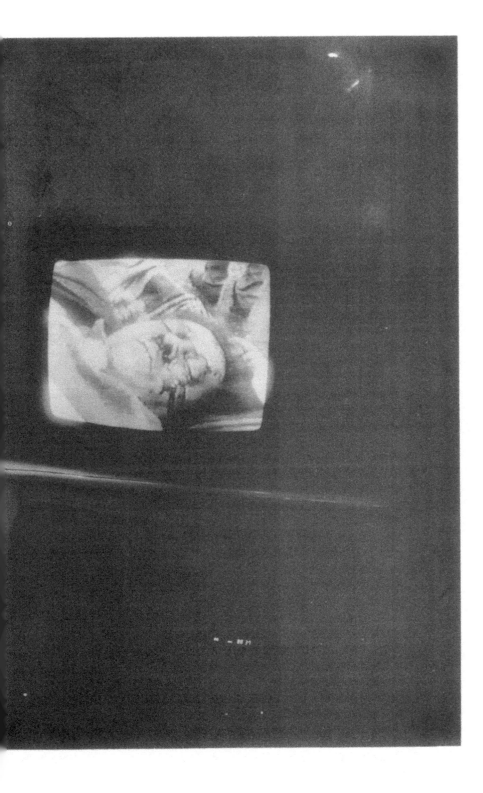

Funeral of Merab Kostava

VICTORIA
TOKAREVA
CENTRE OF
GRAVITY

For reasons I don't want to go into, I decided to commit suicide.

The poet Marshak has these marvellous lines: '*Death came like a court order and seized possession of life.*' Death came to me, too, like a court order. I chose not to resist the summons.

Having no experience with suicide, I turned to fiction. Emma Bovary poisoned herself. As far as I remember from Flaubert, it was a long and painful process, and—in view of the state of medical science at the time—uncertain. You could be saved and then a letter might be written to the courts: the life of every member of society belongs to society, and you have no right to do violence to public property. So poisoning was unsuitable.

Shooting yourself was not realistic. Pistols had gone out of everyday use. This wasn't the nineteenth century, when every self-respecting person had a gun in the way that nowadays they had a cigarette-lighter or a ball-point pen.

What was the alternative? Hanging yourself was unaesthetic. Jumping out of a window was too frightening. I wanted death to enter unobtrusively, to take me gently by the hand and lead me away, as though to happiness, as though into the arms of a loved one after a long separation. After all, that's what it was. Life was separation from eternity. I came from eternity and would return to it. Life was a pause between two eternities and it was up to me, and no one else, how long that pause was to last.

I asked myself: 'What do I love most of all?'

Most of all I liked to be glad. But no one had ever died of gladness. I also loved sleeping. Perhaps I should die in my sleep?

You could take sleeping pills, but sleeping pills were sold only one dose at a time, and you would have to collect doses for a whole week before you had enough. In a week you might change your mind or be distracted.

There was another way: to fall permanently asleep. That is, to freeze to death. Like the coachman in the song, who was snow-bound in the far-off steppes. Survivors say that at first you feel cold, then warm, then you have blissful dreams.

Please don't think I'm joking or playing some kind of game. I was not feeling at all cheerful—although, to be honest, I was not sad either. I didn't feel sorry for myself. I was in a practical mood. I recalled two lines from Bella Akhmadulina:

Let us endure the death of both of us,
Without a show of pity and without a fuss.

My head was stuffed with lines from modern poetry. I knew whole poems by heart; for example: '*I do not want to know where I can be alone.*' But enough about poetry. I had more serious matters to deal with.

I went into the bathroom, started the shower and stepped in. I stood there long enough to get completely wet, then wrapped myself in a big, fluffy bath-towel and went out on to the balcony. Into thirty degrees below freezing.

I felt as if I had stepped into a bonfire, like Joan of Arc. Extreme cold, apparently, burns you. Very high and very low temperatures produce the same effect. It was unbearable standing there; it was like a fire, but without the smoke. I suspect that the blissful dreams are a lie, but to know for certain you had to wait to see if the blissful dreams came true. To wait you had to be patient. And patience required the right mood. Whatever you were doing, the main thing was always to be in the right mood.

My hair instantly turned into a cluster of glass pipettes, my eyelashes became long, white and fluffy. Up in the black sky, the moon hung like an uncooked pancake. I was leaving, but the moon would stay. People would continue to look up from the earth at the moon, and the pancake would go on lying to them that it was meaningful. The city glittered with lighted windows. Behind each window there was an idiot—or several idiots together.

A sound of clumsy rustling came from one side, as though a bear was trying to climb in. Perhaps this was the start of a blissful dream. But it was nothing of the sort. A hulking man was climbing from the balcony next door over on to mine. A burglar most likely. He'd been robbing the neighbouring flat, but the owners had come back unexpectedly, and now he had to get away. Or perhaps he was a heroic but luckless lover. He had come to see another man's wife and, suddenly surprised by the husband, had decided to risk his life on the balcony rather than risk it in a show-down.

Perhaps he was a murderous maniac. There were such types. For me, personally, the appearance of a murderous maniac was a stroke of luck, because he would greatly speed up my intended move from here to *there*; it would be like taking a taxi. You must agree, though: it's one thing to depart this life by your own efforts and quite another to be shoved out of it against your will, even in a taxi.

I screamed with all my might, although I hadn't much might left.

The robber saw me. I was barefoot, encrusted with ice and wrapped in a towel. He stood there like a lamp-post, with the same degree of cast-iron immobility.

'What are you doing here?' he asked, astonished, in an educated voice.

'And what are *you* doing here?' I asked.

My lips couldn't move, and I spoke the words like a ventriloquist.

'I want to go through your flat on to the staircase. May I?'

'You may,' I said graciously.

'And you?'

'What about me?'

'Won't you see me out? I don't know how your locks work.'

Obviously not a burglar. Otherwise the locks wouldn't have bothered him.

'All right,' I agreed and stepped off the balcony into my room.

The light was on. I hadn't turned it off before dying. My towel had frozen and was like a sheet of tin.

The robber followed me and was clearly baffled.

'What were you doing out there?' he inquired, overcome by curiosity.

'It was too hot in here.'

'Do you practise yoga?'

'Yes,' I agreed; it saved explanations.

'Aren't you cold?'

'No. I'm used to it.'

We went to the front door. With rigid fingers I opened the lock and, before letting the robber out, I turned and looked at him. Again I felt a burning sensation, as I had from the cold. I recognized him.

'Are you Onisimov?'

'No, I'm not Onisimov. Who's he?'

'Oh . . . just somebody.'

Onisimov was my first love. I was fourteen. Our school was across the street from a student hostel, and the windows of our classroom overlooked a room occupied by two jolly students. During break-time the girls would hang over the window-sill and shout stupid, cheerful things at the boys below. One was Onisimov; he actually shouted out: 'I'm Onisimov!' He had blond hair, nice regular features, long arms and strong hands. I've always remembered him.

Love for Onisimov went into my heart like a needle of happiness, but I didn't show my love in any way. I never hung over the window-sill and shouted. I stood behind the others and stared, unable to tear myself away. No doubt he never saw me. Or had an inkling of my love.

In class I would sit with my neck twisted, looking out at Onisimov's window. Sometimes he would appear briefly, and then my heart turned a somersault, gently detaching itself as though in a state of weightlessness, and floated down to my stomach. I almost fainted.

When I moved up the next year, our windows looked out on the other side of the building. It all ended. We never got to know each other, he never had a chance to disappoint me and my love for him remained imperishable. Like the honey in the sarcophagus. Recently they dug up a pharaoh from the depths of several millennia. Not even the pharaoh's buttons had survived, but an amphora of honey was still intact. You could have sat down and had it for tea. Such was my love for Onisimov.

I can't say I've waited for him all my life. He couldn't have come to me, because he didn't know me. In those days the queen of the window-sill was Rita Nosikova, a red-haired beauty, while I stood at the back wearing spectacles, with my stockings twisted, my head stuffed with poetry. He didn't see me, and naturally never guessed at my love. But I remember him; he was part of my life. And the fact that he had appeared at precisely this fateful moment was on the one hand improbable, but on the other—entirely natural.

'No. I am not Onisimov,' he repeated. 'People are always mixing me up with somebody else. I always seem to look like another person.'

He really was like Onisimov, but I could have been mistaken.

A lot of water had flowed under the bridge since I was fourteen. And I had seen Onisimov only from a distance, across the street. I looked at the man's hands. Hands like his could never steal or kill, but they might caress.

'Well, goodbye,' said Not-Onisimov. 'Please excuse me.'

I shut the door after him. I didn't want to return to the balcony. The mood had gone.

I went into the bathroom, ran a bathful of hot water, got into it and began slowly to thaw out, like a chicken taken out of the freezer. The warmth went into me gradually, in layers, penetrating deeper as I bathed. I felt the warmth as if it were happiness—so real, I could have touched it with my hand.

Having thawed out, I reached for some Green Apple shampoo, washed my hair and dried it with a hand drier. The stream of hot air blew around my face. I scraped off some old nail varnish with my finger-nail and gave myself a fresh manicure. I put on my wedding-dress: white embroidery on white muslin. It was made out of Yugoslav curtain-material and had been incredibly expensive when I bought it, though today the price would be reasonable. I had worn it once in my life, for my wedding. Since then it had been hanging in my wardrobe like an exhibit in a museum of ethnography, a reflection of my history and my glorious past.

Having dressed myself like a bride, I took an opened bottle of champagne out of the refrigerator, sat down at the kitchen table and turned on the gas taps—all four burners and the oven. There was a strong smell of garlic. My head seemed to fill with gas and felt light.

Don't think I'm mad. I was simply like an aeroplane that had run out of fuel and had started to glide. Its centre of gravity was displaced and it went into a dive. That was my state at the time. I was outside myself.

I poured out some champagne and drank. The walls of the kitchen shuddered and started going round in a slow waltz rhythm, with heavy stress on one beat. I wanted to get up and circle in time with the walls. I heard a ring at the door. I decided the ringing was in my ears, but ringing in your ears never sounds so insistent and panicky. The ringing stopped and I heard knocking: fists were hammering on the door, feet kicking it; then someone stepped back, took a run and hit it with his whole body. I realized that if I didn't get up at once and open it, my door would come crashing down.

I went into the hall, slid back the bolts and took off the chain. On the threshold stood Not-Onisimov. He saw me in the white dress and went as rigid as a lamp-post for the second time. Then he firmly pushed me aside and marched into the kitchen, as though he were not a caller but in his own home. Not-Onisimov turned off all the gas taps and flung open the window. Frosty air strode into the kitchen; it was too heavy to float in.

'Why did you turn on the gas?' Not-Onisimov asked sternly.

'I was trying to get warm,' I replied.

'One moment you're too hot, the next you're too cold,' he said, displeased.

'What business is it of yours? Why are you shuttling in and out of here? First you come in by the window, then by the door.'

'Because I don't like the look of you.' He stared me straight in the eye, and I took off my glasses so that I wouldn't see him clearly. 'Why are you behaving like this? Has somebody upset you?'

'I don't ask *you* questions like this.'

'You can if you like.'

'Why were you escaping over the balcony? Did her husband come?'

'Yes.' Not-Onisimov confirmed my suspicion, nodding his head. 'How did you know?'

'From all those jokes. Typical situation. He arrived—and at the wrong time.'

'Yes. We hadn't made any arrangement.'

'Obviously. You don't have to explain.'

'I didn't want to see him. The fact is, I've killed his wife.'

This was an unexpected twist to the typical situation. I put on my glasses, and having refocused I looked at my uninvited visitor. 'Out of jealousy?' I inquired.

'I'm a doctor. Surgeon. I operated on her.'

'Ah, I see . . . A botched job.'

'Botched job? It was the operation of the century! Only De Baeky has done one like it! Have you heard of De Baeky?'

'No,' I confessed.

Not-Onisimov looked at me with contempt, as though De Baeky were Shakespeare. Incidentally, I haven't read Shakespeare.

I see his plays in the theatre.

'De Baeky is the foremost surgeon in the world. He proposed implanting a Teflon valve into the heart. All valves before him were ball-and-socket. The ball functioned well enough, but it made such a noise that the patient sounded like a clock. You could hear it ticking from five metres away. Then there were the so-called petal valves. Later they tried implanting the valve from a pig's heart. De Baeky was the first to suggest Teflon. Do you know what Teflon is?'

'No.'

'You don't know anything. It's a super-durable synthetic material. It's used in non-stick frying-pans, it lets you fry without fat. A Teflon valve will never wear out.'

'Like one's first love,' I thought. If De Baeky had operated on that pharaoh, they would have found a valve as well as the honey.

'Did you sew a valve like that into her?' I asked, guessing.

'I didn't sew it in. I glued it in. I went further than De Baeky. For five years I've been working with a group of scientists to develop an organic glue that is gradually absorbed by the body's tissues. The valve settles in without a single stitch and without any traumatic effect on the heart muscles. But the chief advantage is time. A valve implant used to take five hours. Now it takes forty minutes. Like taking out an appendix. I have advanced surgery by a hundred years. I have practically relieved people of the fear of heart disease. We'll be able to mend hearts the way we mend cars in a repair workshop. I phoned De Baeky. He's invited me to see him, along with my patient. But the trouble is, she's not recovering.'

'Why not?'

'She's not fighting. She says she's tired. When a person doesn't want to live, it's fatal. Because it's all up here.' Not-Onisimov tapped his forehead. 'I once had a case in which I operated on a very severe ulcer. I was convinced it wouldn't be successful. The patient was a lorry-driver, who drove a refrigerated truck full of fish. He used to swallow fish whole, like a cat. And he drank, in my opinion . . . But that's not the point. I was afraid he'd die on the operating-table. But he didn't. I completed the operation. An hour later I went to see him in the resuscitation unit, and his bed was empty. I looked under the bed; I thought he might have fallen out. He wasn't there. The attendants ran around looking for him. I went into the toilet—and there he was, sitting and smoking. His brain hadn't taken in the seriousness of the operation. Believe it or not, he recovered. But this woman's case . . . In America an operation like hers would cost one and a half million dollars.'

Not-Onisimov poured himself some champagne and drank it. 'Want some?' he asked me, although it was I and not he who should have offered it.

'Thanks.' I sat down at the table.

Not-Onisimov sat down too; he didn't drink any more, but leaned his head on his hand, looking mournful. I noticed the bald patch on the crown of his head and a needle of pity went into my heart.

'It's not your fault,' I said with conviction. 'You've done everything you could. But if she . . . It's up to her now.'

'There's no such thing as an operation in the abstract, detached from the patient. It's much better for a patient to survive after a bad operation than for him or her to die after a good operation . . . And her husband came to say thank you. Brought me a bottle of brandy. French.'

'So that's *your* flat next door?' I was amazed.

'Of course. I live on the staircase next to yours.'

'I've never seen you.'

'I've never seen you, either.'

'So the husband is still there, sitting in your flat.'

'I don't know. Probably.'

'But why couldn't you have gone out by the door?'

'Well, it's awkward to walk out when someone comes to see you. So I just disappeared. Without any explanations.'

'Yes, but even so, it's an awkward situation. You'll have to go back.'

'I've got to be at the hospital.'

I didn't understand. 'What's the time?'

'Doesn't matter. I must be near her. Or rather, I can't let myself be anywhere else.'

'Well, go then . . .'

'I can't leave you.'

'Why not?'

'I've told you: I don't like the look of you.'

'But you can't be in two places at once.'

'Will you come with me?' asked Not-Onisimov.

99

I put on a leather coat over my wedding-dress, took off my gilded slippers and stuck my feet into a pair of felt boots. Not-Onisimov was wearing only a sweater and jeans.

'Can't I give you something to wear for the cold?' I asked.

'What have you got?'

'Nothing. I haven't got any men's clothes.'

'In that case I'll take a blanket,' said Not-Onisimov, inventively. 'Do you have any blankets?'

I had two bed-covers, an eiderdown and a quilt. I gave him the eiderdown. Not-Onisimov wrapped himself to the top of his head. He looked very good in the eiderdown.

The hospital consisted of a group of white buildings, like doctors' white coats, and we entered one and climbed the stairs to the second floor.

'Why do you have to replace people's heart-valves?' I asked.

'The old one breaks down. When I saw her valve, I couldn't understand why she was still alive.'

'Why do they break down?'

'Not "they"; it. The mitral valve. Between the auricle and the ventricle.'

'But why do they break down? From stress?'

'From rheumatoid assault.'

'Assault? What's that?'

'You're not a doctor. You wouldn't understand.'

We walked into an office. Not-Onisimov threw my eiderdown on to a couch and took a white coat out of the cupboard and left the room, only to return immediately. 'Come with me!' he commanded. He was obviously afraid of leaving me alone.

A dim light was burning in the corridor. It was deserted. The patients were asleep. *'Silent, still as water in a bowl, life lay sleeping.'* I've left out 'her'. It should be: 'Her *life lay sleeping.'*

She was not asleep. She was in a single-bed room, staring at the ceiling. It was impossible to determine her age: somewhere between twenty and fifty. She did not react when we came in.

'Alla!' Not-Onisimov called out her name.

She continued staring upwards.

Not-Onisimov lifted her limp arm from her chest and took her pulse, then put her arm back.

'Alla!' Not-Onisimov said quietly. 'Please.'

Alla didn't hear. Or didn't want to hear. She conveyed the cold indifference of outer space.

Not-Onisimov tried to say something but couldn't. He turned around and went out of the room like a blind man. I had the feeling that he would burst into tears. He had forgotten me in his despair. A needle of pity went right through me.

'Please . . .' I repeated softly.

I sat down on the bed in such a way as to interrupt her gaze, to catch her eye. She saw me in my white wedding-dress and felt boots and evidently concluded that it was Death who had appeared in this strange garb, but not even Death aroused her interest.

'I understand you,' I whispered fervently. 'I understand . . . You've been in so much pain, I don't know how you kept on living. You're tired and you want to rest at any cost. Even at the cost of falling asleep for ever. You want a rest from pain, from people, from everything that life is, because your life is nothing but heart aches. No one can suffer so long. You've had too much. Your spring has broken. I understand. But you're not alone, Alla. Your doctor, who has mended you, is on your side. Hundreds, thousands of patients who need your recovery as a guarantee—they're all praying for you. And Dr De Baeky is on your side too, and the whole of America; they're cheering for you. People get sick there too, you know. In America an operation like yours costs a million and a half dollars. Only a millionaire can afford it, and not even every millionaire. Yours was done free. And still you're . . . being obstinate. Maybe you don't care for the rest of the human race any longer—you may not care about America or De Baeky. But the people who love you are backing you up. Right now your husband can't sleep; he's going out of his mind. You simply haven't the right. Can you hear me?'

'Who are you?' Alla asked softly.

'No one,' I said.

'I'm not dreaming about you, am I?'

'No. I exist. I'm real.'

I bent low over Alla and my glasses fell off on to her face. She raised her hand, picked up my glasses and put them on.

'You really are there,' she breathed. 'I can see you now.' She could see and hear me, and her attention sent a cold shiver through me. I had completely forgotten about my troubles and about my reasons (which I don't want to tell you about) for standing on the balcony.

'You mustn't think of only yourself. You mustn't love only yourself or pity yourself. Otherwise your centre of gravity will be upset.'

'What will be upset?' asked Alla.

'Everything. The whole solar system. You don't have the right.'

'What do you want me to do?' Alla asked weakly.

'I only want you to go to the lavatory.'

'What for?'

'To have a smoke.'

'I don't want to. I can't.'

'But you don't know whether you can or not. People don't know their own potential.'

I put my arms round Alla's shoulders and started to lift her up. She clasped my neck and let me guide her.

'My valve won't come loose, will it?' Alla asked. She was afraid for her life, and that was a good sign.

'No, it won't,' I assured her. 'But it'll get a bit of a surprise.'

She was up. We walked slowly out of the room and into the corridor, I with my white wedding-dress, Alla in her white patient's gown with the hospital stamp on the back. We clutched each other like a pair of white ghosts, and I had the feeling that if we were to jump in the air we would take off and float. Her weakness flowed into me, and my gladness flowed into her, the gladness that I love more than anything else on earth and would like to die of. But at that moment I didn't want to die. My earlier mood had gone, vanished. I wanted only one thing: to keep walking with Alla, my arms around her, to carry this stranger's fragile life, like a butterfly, in the palm of my hand.

The corridor was empty. A nurse was dozing on a sofa. An alarm clock was giving out a hypnotic tick and the sound, like a cricket's song, carried through the corridors.

Not-Onisimov emerged from the office where he had dressed. He saw us and did his lamp-post act again.

'Good evening,' Alla greeted him, although it was almost morning.

'What are you doing here?' was all that Not-Onisimov could think of saying.

'We're going for a smoke,' I said.

Not-Onisimov dashed towards us, took Alla's arm and felt her pulse. Then he turned to me, with an astonished look on his face, and asked: 'How did you do it?'

The alarm clock rang. It was six o'clock in the morning. Time for the first injections.

The nurse got up from the sofa. She was a broad-hipped, broad-shouldered girl in round spectacles. She looked like a denizen of the forest, like the strange, fairy-tale creature Ukhti-Tukhti. I had heard the story as a child, but to this day I have never understood who or what Ukhti-Tukhti was. A chicken, perhaps, or a hedgehog.

'Here,' ordered Not-Onisimov. The taxi-driver stopped the car outside Not-Onisimov's entrance.

'I must sleep,' Not-Onisimov explained as he paid off the cab. 'I haven't slept for five days. I'm going to bed now and I shall sleep like a corpse.'

We clambered out of the taxi. The driver looked at Not-Onisimov in his eiderdown with utter amazement. I wondered what he was thinking. I moved towards my entrance.

'Where are you going?' Not-Onisimov called out. 'Come up to my place.'

He called me as one calls a dog, and I went up to him like a dog, with the same degree of trust and ingenuity.

'But you're going to bed,' I reminded him.

'Well, so what? You can go to bed too. We've even got your eiderdown with us. So you can go to sleep under it.' Not-Onisimov took me by the hand and led the way.

'I can't sleep without a night-dress,' I objected, weakly.

'Can't help you there. Haven't got any women's things. Go to bed in the dress you're wearing.'

We went into the lift. Not-Onisimov leaned back against the rail, shut his eyes and fell asleep standing up, like a horse. I pressed the necessary button. I knew the floor, because we were neighbours and lived on the same level.

I guided Not-Onisimov to his front door. Not being fully awake, he tried to open it but the key wouldn't turn in the lock. 'What the hell?' said Not-Onisimov, puzzled.

I heard a rustling from inside. The door swung open. A tousled, red-shirted man of indeterminate age stood on the threshold. I guessed he was Alla's husband. He might have been thirty or he might have been fifty. Either he was thirty and was looking bad, which was natural in his situation, or he was pushing fifty and looking very good.

'Are you still here?' said Not-Onisimov, not sounding surprised.

'Where else should I be?' The husband sounded surprised.

They were silent for a moment and looked at each other.

'Come in,' said the husband. 'Take off your things.'

We went in. I took off my coat, Not-Onisimov threw off the eiderdown and rubbed his wooden-stiff fingers. His expression was one of exhaustion and happiness. He looked satisfied, like the legendary hero Alyosha Popovich after doing battle with the Tartars.

'Let's have that brandy of yours,' said Not-Onisimov grandly. 'We can drink it now. We have the right. We've earned it.'

'But I'm afraid I've already drunk it,' said the husband, embarrassed. 'You were away for so long.'

'All of it?' Not-Onisimov was dismayed.

'Well, yes,' the husband confirmed guiltily. 'I waited and waited.'

'In that case you can go home,' said Not-Onisimov, dismissing him. He rubbed his hands like a man of action. Not-Onisimov had operated successfully. Not-Onisimov's life was a success. No more and no less. 'Go home,' he said.

'Me?' the husband countered, prodding his red-checked chest with his index finger.

'Both of you.' He turned to me. 'You too. Go and get undressed in your normal way and you will sleep normally. It's uncomfortable sleeping in your clothes, anyway.'

'Why are you kicking me out?'

'Because I don't like the look of you.'

He came up to me. Took off my glasses. Began to survey my short-sighted features as though stroking me with his eyes. My heart turned a somersault, gently detaching itself from its moorings, and floated in a state of weightlessness.

'I think I've seen you somewhere before.'

'Of course you have. We're neighbours, after all.'

'No. Before that.'

Perhaps when I had been standing behind the other girls. Behind Rita Nosikova's broad, laughing face.

'I don't want to go all the way downstairs and all the way up again. Can I go out over your balcony?'

'You can,' allowed Not-Onisimov. 'But I'll help you.'

We went on to the balcony. He offered me his strong, handsome, talented hand. I leaned against it and confidently climbed up to the balcony rail. The city was asleep and dreaming its pre-dawn dreams.

How many times in my life have I stretched out my hand in help, and to how many people, I wonder? And when I have needed help, none of them have ever been around. The one who did happen to be around was a total stranger, who by chance dropped—literally—at my feet. Therefore the principle of 'You scratch my back, I'll scratch yours' doesn't work, because goodness is unselfish. You help me, I'll help someone else, he'll help another person—and so on through time and space. Let the chain not be broken.

Alla's husband came out on to the balcony too and solicitously draped my eiderdown around Not-Onisimov. The husband was taking care of Not-Onisimov. Not-Onisimov was supporting me. I had supported Alla. Alla was all mankind, and mankind, God willing, would stretch out a hand to her husband. And then the whole world would be joined up in a single Grand Chain.

The sky was lighting up, the black turning to grey, and the moon, having lost the chic dark background which showed it off so well, had faded and was neutral, uninteresting—neither good nor bad. The houses looked like a photographic negative: the walls were light, the windows dark. And it seemed to me that behind each window there slept a genius, or even several geniuses together.

Translated from the Russian by Michael Glenny.

LUDMILLA
PETRUSHEVSKAYA
OUR CIRCLE

I am afraid that my memory is confused about these events, the final events of my life, by which I mean what happened before I started to go blind. But in the beginning it was like this: every Friday we went to Serge and Marisha's—as though magnetized by their little house on Stulina Street—and drank all night.

It was always the same people; if someone didn't turn up it was because of circumstances at home or because they were out of favour with Marisha and the others. For ages they wouldn't have Andrei because once when he was drunk he had punched Serge in the eye: at the time we regarded Serge as untouchable; he was our pride and show-piece. (He was a rising star in the scientific world.) Usually, though, there were Serge and Marisha; and their daughter, Sonya, in the next room. Then there was myself—there for no good reason—and my husband Kolya; Andrei the Stool-Pigeon (so-called because once he had agreed to be an informer for the authorities so that he could go on a Pacific expedition), first with his wife, then with various other women, later with his steady girl-friend Nadya; Zhora, who was half-Jewish from his mother (a fact which no one—apart from me—ever mentioned), was there and, like many small men, displayed a permanent state of arousal. And Tanya, a six-foot Valkyrie, with long blonde hair and very white teeth which she cleaned obsessively three times a day, for twenty minutes at a time. She was Serge's favourite: he would sometimes stroke her hair when he was very drunk and thought nobody was noticing, and his wife Marisha would sit quietly as if nothing was wrong.

And then there was Lenka Marchukaite, a very pretty girl of twenty with a double-D cup bra. Lenka behaved like a black-market operator. She wormed her way into Marisha's confidence by telling her how difficult her life was, scrounged twenty roubles and disappeared. When Lenka returned, her four front teeth were missing. She paid back the twenty roubles (Marisha was triumphant) and said she had been in hospital, where they had told her that she could never have children. Marisha liked her all the more. Before that, Lenka had never been invited to stay the night at Marisha's flat, but without her front teeth it was a different matter. With Serge's help, Lenka got a job and had four false teeth put in. Afterwards, whenever she came into a room, she picked out one of the men and sat down on his lap while the other poor boys—my husband Kolya or Andrei the Stool-Pigeon—grinned awkwardly. Once she sat on Kolya's lap. My Kolya, thin and good-natured, was crushed by Lenka's weight. He kept his hands away from her and cast imploring looks at Marisha, but Marisha turned away sharply and started talking to Zhora. Seeing that, I understood something. I said: 'Lenka, you've made a silly mistake. Marisha is jealous of you making up to my husband.'

Lenka light-heartedly pulled a face but remained on Kolya's lap, while he went as limp as a plucked flower-stalk. This, I think, was the beginning of Marisha's cooling-off towards Lenka Marchukaite, which led to Lenka's gradual disappearance. On this occasion, though, everyone reacted with a burst of exaggerated activity. Tanya clinked glasses with Serge, Zhora poured out more vodka and Andrei the Stool Pigeon gallantly started talking to his silly little girl-friend, who looked triumphantly at me, the wife of the crushed husband.

Lenka Marchukaite, however, never risked sitting on Zhora. Once one of Andrei's ladies had pretended to be terribly hot-blooded when dancing with Zhora. When the music stopped Zhora simply lifted her by the armpits and dragged her, apparently unconscious, into the next room. Zhora managed to heave the dazed lady on to Sonya's little bed (Sonya was staying with her grandmother) but Serge and Andrei, laughing despite themselves, appeared and dragged him off her, while the alarmed lady pulled down her dress, which had been yanked up above her waist. The incident provoked laughter all that night, although everyone, except the lady in question, who was an outsider, knew it was all a game: ever since his student days Zhora had played the Don Juan, whereas in fact he spent his nights writing his wife's dissertation and always got up to attend to his three children.

Ten or maybe fifteen years I spent going to those Fridays. The news from Czechoslovakia, Poland, China, Yugoslavia flashed by. The trials of various dissidents took place, followed by the trials of those who had protested at the outcome of the first trials, then the trials of those who had collected money in aid of the families of dissidents incarcerated in labour camps—it all passed us by. Only occasionally did the outside world intrude, as when migrant birds from other, adjoining areas came flying into our circle. The front door of the flat, just three steps up from the street, was never shut on Fridays. Our local policeman, Valera, took to coming. The first time he came was in connection with a complaint, lodged by the tenants of the house across the street, about the excessive noise we had been making. Valera carefully checked everyone's documents, or rather he checked to see whether we had them on us, because it turned out that not one of the men was carrying his ID card. He didn't check the women, which subsequently made us think that Valera was looking for someone specific. For the whole of the next week everyone was terribly worried and we all exchanged frequent, nervous telephone calls. A hint of danger had penetrated our quiet little backwater; thanks to Valera we were suddenly adrift in the mainstream of events.

By the following Friday, everyone assumed for certain that Valera was looking for Levka, a Russian-American who had been living in Moscow for a year with an expired visa. Levka was in hiding—everyone welcomed him with much noise and laughter—and though I never saw him at Marisha's place, he had sometimes slept on her neighbour's floor.

That night, however, Valera turned up again at five past eleven to silence the music from our tape-recorder. We switched it off and sat drinking in silence. Valera, for no detectable reason, stayed there: either he had decided to wait just in case Levka did show up, or he wanted to give our harmless little gathering a thoroughly hard time. Marisha used to argue hotly that all people without exception were interesting—she was always giving beds for the night to people she met at railway stations; once, for a whole month she had housed a woman who brought her year-old, paralysed baby girl for out-patient consultations at a nearby paediatric clinic—and she began holding animated conversation with Valera on various subjects, gave him a glass of dry wine and offered him bread and cheese. Valera did not evade a single question.

Serge joined in, saying: 'Why did you join the police? To get a Moscow residence-permit?'

'No, I already had a permit,' Valera replied.

'What's the job like?'

'Tough district, this,' said Valera. 'I learned unarmed combat when I was in the army, but I never made Second Class because I had my shoulder dislocated. When you're training, if someone gets you in a lock that's going to do you an injury, you have to give an audible signal.'

'What sort of audible signal?' I asked.

'Well, you should cough, or—pardon the expression—you could fart, so as to stop him breaking your arm.'

I asked how it was possible to fart to order.

Valera replied that he personally hadn't managed to give a loud enough audible signal in time to stop his opponent from dislocating his shoulder; that was why he had only made it to Third Class in unarmed combat. Then, without drawing breath, he gave his views on the current state of the nation, telling us how everything was going to change soon and it would be like it was under Stalin, because there had been law and order under Stalin.

For all of us, in one way or another, that Friday was torture. Not once did Lenka Marchukaite sit on anyone's lap—least of all on Valera's—nor did Zhora call out through the window at the passing schoolgirls. I kept asking how unarmed combat enthusiasts learned the technique of making 'audible signals': was it by will-power, or by eating special food? I managed to make that theme last for the whole evening. It was the only topic that Valera avoided.

Like Cinderellas, we all got up and left on the stroke of midnight—but not Valera. Either he had nowhere else to spend his spell of night-duty or he had some specific assignment, but he stayed with Marisha and Serge until morning. After Marisha had retired to sleep on the floor in Sonya's room, Serge had manfully stayed to drink herbal tea with Valera, a whole teapotful made with St John's wort, a powerful diuretic. Valera had achieved a miracle of continence, obviously determined not to leave his observation-post for a second. Serge, for his part, hadn't left the room either, fearing the policeman might search the place while he was out.

That night my Kolya and I didn't lash out on a taxi but caught a bus home like normal people, to find that at one-thirty in the morning our son Alyosha wasn't asleep but was sitting in a daze in front of the television. The screen was blank. This was the first Friday that we had returned at night and not in the morning, and we realized that Friday nights had also been a sort of holiday for Alyosha. When I was putting him to bed he said he was afraid of sleeping alone and had been too frightened to put out the light. The lights were on everywhere.

I've already mentioned that a good few years flowed past our Fridays. From being a golden-haired young Paris, Andrei became in turn a father; an abandoned husband; a stool-pigeon on a scientific expedition abroad; a lawful husband again and prospective owner of a nice co-operative flat bought for Nadya by her father; and, finally, an alcoholic. Marisha was still the only real love of Andrei's life, as she had been since their student days. He lived for his dances with her—one or two sacramental dances each year.

Zhora grew from being a student prankster into a modest, poverty-stricken Senior Research Fellow, wearing the cheapest of shirts and dark-grey trousers. He became the father of three children and no doubt would be a future Lenin Prize winner. But there had always been something else about him: he also loved Marisha.

They had all lost their heads over Marisha in their first year at university. In those days our life had been made up of long hikes and seaside camp-fires. We drank dry wine and were sarcastic about absolutely everything. Serge had been one of the many to fall in love with Marisha and—after establishing his manliness by doggedly catching fish with a harpoon—had proposed to her and slept with her. At night I heard the rhythmic pounding coming from their tent, but Marisha was always restless (not a good advertisement for Serge's abilities as a lover), and all the other boys were straining to fill the gap, as it were. In fact, this sexual fire which consumed Marisha, our priestess of love, combined with her inaccessibility, was what enabled our whole group to stick together for so long. We, the girls, loved Serge; at the same time we loved Marisha. On the one hand we wanted to make love to Serge and dreamed of replacing Marisha, on the other hand we could never make love to Serge, out of sympathy, love and pity for Marisha. In other words, everything was dominated by Marisha and Serge: they were our common bond.

This game went on until last New Year's Eve's party, when we had all drunk a lot, and Serge, who had then been married to Marisha for many years, got up and said: 'I'm going to phone the love of my life.' She was a girl he had known from his schooldays and recently met on the street where he had lived as a child. According to several well-informed persons she was now a fat brunette, but Serge had rediscovered his youthful erotic dream.

Several knots then unravelled. Serge stopped sleeping at home with Marisha. Our Fridays ceased to take place, although other Fridays were sometimes held on neutral ground—for instance in the flat of Tanya the Valkyrie, although Tanya's teenage son was morbidly jealous of anyone friendly with his mother and so had to be sent away to spend Friday nights at Stulina Street with young Sonya, Marisha's daughter. I remarked that it did children good to sleep together, but nobody paid me any attention. There was more to follow. Marisha's father called on Serge one night to have a man-to-man talk and ask him why he was leaving Marisha; but he drank too much, talked a lot of pointless nonsense and was equally pointlessly killed by a car in Stulina Street, on the threshold of his daughter's house, at the quiet evening hour of half past nine. At this time, too, my mother's life was gently coming to its end. She had dwindled from eighty to twenty-seven kilograms. Towards the very end the doctors took it into their heads to look for a non-existent ulcer inside her. So they opened her up, by mistake sewed her intestine to her peritoneum and left her to die with an open surgical wound the size of your fist. My husband Kolya took no part in this. He and I had been formally divorced five years before, except that neither of us had paid for the divorce, having agreed simply to continue living together as husband and wife with no claims on each other. We just went on living like everyone else, until one day he went and paid for the divorce. After my mother's funeral he calmly suggested I should pay my half too, which I did. Then, three months later, when I got up in the night to cover Alyosha with his blanket, I noticed that my father wasn't breathing. I went back to bed, slept until morning, took Alyosha to school and then my father to the hospital morgue.

All that happened between Fridays, and I missed several of them. A month later it was Easter. Every Easter everyone gathered at our flat. My mother, father and I used to prepare lots of food, then my parents would take Alyosha on the ninety-minute train journey to our allotment, where they burned last year's leaves, tidied and cleaned and then the three of them would sleep there, in the unheated hut, enabling my guests to eat, drink and be merry all night.

This year I was determined that everything was to be the same. In the morning I told Alyosha that he was to take the train out to the allotment and spend the night there by himself: there was no other solution; he was a big boy now—he was seven—and he knew the way perfectly well. I warned him that on no account was he to return that night. So he set off, before his afternoon nap, on the trip out to the allotment, while I began making pastry for the cabbage pie. I couldn't afford much more. Cabbage pie, pasties filled with my mother's home-made jam, potato salad, hard-boiled eggs with spring onions, grated beetroot with mayonnaise, a little cheese, some sliced salami and a bottle of vodka.

The fact is I don't earn much and I couldn't expect Kolya to contribute because he had almost completely moved out. On his rare visits he would shout at Alyosha that he wasn't eating properly, that he shouldn't hiccup like that, that he was sitting wrongly, that he was dropping crumbs on the floor, that he was growing into God knows what, that he never read anything, never drew anything, simply did nothing. His impotent shrieking at Alyosha was a cry of jealousy evoked by Marisha's daughter Sonya, who sang, composed music, was a pupil at a special school for gifted children where only one in 300 applicants was accepted, had read since the age of two and could write poetry and fairy-tales. At heart, Kolya loved Alyosha but he would have loved him much more if the child had been talented and good-looking, had done well at school and had been popular among his class-mates. As it was, he saw himself in the boy and it drove him to fury, especially when Alyosha was eating. Alyosha had bad teeth. He was a messy eater and took big mouthfuls without chewing them properly, dropped food and drink on his trousers, was always spilling things—and to cap it all he had started wetting his bed at night. I believe the reason why Kolya shot out of our family—suddenly, like a cork out of a bottle—was to avoid seeing his urine-soaked son, his little thin legs trembling in wet pyjama trousers. The first time Kolya found the boy in that disgraceful state, having been woken up by his crying, he gave Alyosha a resounding slap across the cheek and Alyosha fell gently back on to his wet, sour-smelling bed. I left and went to work, leaving them to sort themselves out. I had an eye examination that day, which revealed the first stages of the hereditary disease that had killed my mother. Or rather, the doctor, who would not give a conclusive diagnosis, prescribed the same drops that mother had been given and ordered the same tests. So now it was all starting with me, too, as if it wasn't enough that Alyosha was wetting his bed and Kolya had hit him. I came home to find Kolya's personal belongings gone, although he did have the decency to leave everything else behind.

Anyway, for Easter I baked pies, moved the table out from the wall, covered it with a table-cloth, laid out plates, glasses, salad, salami, cheese and bread—there were even a few apples, a present from one of mother's friends who had brought me a bag of them, rare enough in spring—and some painted eggs. My annual guests all arrived together, slightly embarrassed: Marisha would not have missed coming for anything, and the rest came because of her—including Serge and Kolya. Kolya went straight into the kitchen to unload everything they had brought, which included baked potatoes with dill cucumbers and enough wine to keep us going all night. And why shouldn't they have looked forward to a good party? Here was someone else's empty flat, plus a nicely piquant situation: my ex-husband Kolya and Marisha had married the day before. How would I react?

Andrei the Stool-Pigeon put on a record. Tanya the Valkyrie sailed in, teeth and eyes flashing. I asked her whether they had put her boy and Sonya to sleep in the same room, which would be nice for them. Tanya replied, as usual, by neighing gently, showing even more of her enormous teeth. I then asked what the two children might be up to, there in the same room.

'*That's* what they're doing,' Tanya answered cheerfully.

'It's all right for you,' I said, 'yours is a boy, but it's worse for Marisha. Marisha, have you taught Sonya to take precautions?'

'Don't worry, I have,' said Marisha, refusing to join in with Tanya's suppressed mirth. Marisha was angry.

Serge and Zhora came out of the kitchen, already quite drunk, and Kolya emerged from what had once been our bedroom.

'Kolya, have you got a better pair of sheets for yourself?' I asked and realized that my question was right on target.

Kolya shook his head.

'Marisha, have you and my husband got anything to sleep on? I understand you divided up the sheets between Serge and yourself.

115

All my sheets were ruined when Kolya decided he would wash the linen for the first time in his life and threw it into boiling water, stewing all the stains so that they emerged as great clouds all over the sheets.'

At this everyone burst into general, friendly laughter and sat down to table. I had finished playing my role; it was then that Serge showed that he, too, was played out. In rambling, thick-tongued, nasal tones he began arguing with Zhora about the General Field Theory of someone called Ryabkin; Serge furiously attacked Ryabkin, while Zhora tolerantly defended him, then pretended to capitulate reluctantly and agreed with Serge. There, for the first time, Serge showed the signs of a failed scientist, of a man who wasn't going to make it in his field, while also for the first time the modest Zhora revealed himself as the new rising scientific star, because there is no surer sign of personal success than condescending tolerance to colleagues.

'When do you defend your doctoral dissertation, Zhora?' I asked. Zhora took the bait and replied immediately that the 'trial run' would be on Tuesday and the defence proper would be when his turn came up in the queue.

Everyone was silent for a moment, then started drinking. They drank until they were in a state of near-stupor, but the talk around the table refused to take off. Kolya and Marisha were speaking to each other quietly, and I knew what they were whispering about: Marisha wanted Kolya to collect the rest of his belongings.

'Marisha, do you like my flat?' I asked. 'Maybe you might move in here, and Alyosha and I will go and live somewhere else—in fact wherever you suggest. The boy and I don't need much, and you can have our things.'

'You fool,' said Andrei loudly.

'But why not? Have them!' I said. 'I don't need much and Alyosha's going to a children's home. I've already started making the arrangements. It's in Borovsk.'

'Any more brilliant suggestions?' said Kolya.

'Come on, let's get out of here, I can't stand these scenes,' said Andrei the Stool-Pigeon. He made a determined move to get up, together with his Nadya, but none of the others budged: they wanted to see how this would end.

'Yes, I'm fixing a place for him in a children's home. Here are the application forms.' Without getting up, I produced the questionnaire and completed forms.

Kolya looked at them and tore them up.

Andrei put on another record, and Serge went over to his ex-wife Marisha and invited her to dance. Marisha blushed scarlet. It was good to see the furtive look she threw at me—yes, at me! 'It seems I've already become the group's conscience,' I muttered as I put the cabbage pie on the table.

At that point the party really got going; it became a celebration of our affection for each other.

Kolya, who was playing wallflower, came over and asked: 'Where's Alyosha?'

'I don't know,' I said. 'Out somewhere.'

'But it's one o'clock in the morning!' Kolya said and then disappeared into the hall.

I didn't try to stop him, but I knew he hadn't left to put his coat on. He turned into the lavatory and was there a long time in silence. Meanwhile Marisha started to feel sick. She had drunk too much and succeeded only in hanging out of the kitchen window and throwing up her entire meal on to the wall below.

Andrei the Stool-Pigeon pulled himself together and sternly collected Nadya; the metro would soon stop running. Serge and Zhora helped each other on with their coats. Kolya came out of the lavatory and, forgetting that this wasn't his home any longer, lay down on the divan, but Zhora picked him up and led him into the hallway. Last of all in the procession was the radiant Tanya. When I finally opened the front door for them, they all saw Alyosha asleep on the top stair.

I jumped out on to the landing, picked him up and, with a furious cry—'Where the hell have you been?', I shouted—I hit my son in the face, making his nose bleed. He was still not awake and he started to choke. I hit him again, then I began hitting him all over. The others threw themselves at me, twisted my arms behind my back, shoved me back into the flat and slammed the door. Someone outside held the door shut, and I hammered on it. I could hear someone sobbing, and Nadya shouting: 'Just let me get my hands on her! God! The bitch!'

And as they went downstairs, Kolya shouted: 'Alyosha! Alyosha! That's enough! I'm taking you with me! Anywhere, but

not back to a mother like that! Anywhere but here! It's monstrous!'
I bolted the door and crept back into the kitchen to look out of
the window, leaning over Marisha's half-digested beetroot salad.
The whole party came spilling out of the front door. Kolya was
carrying Alyosha! It was a full-scale triumphal procession. They
were all talking excitedly and waiting for someone. Last to emerge
was Andrei the Stool-Pigeon; he must have been holding the door.
As he came out, Nadya shouted at him: 'Deprivation of maternal
rights, that's what!' They were all on a high. Marisha was busily
attending to Alyosha with a handkerchief. Their drunken voices
boomed out all over the district. They even succeeded in hailing a
taxi. Kolya and Alyosha, supported by Marisha, stumbling, eased
themselves on to the back seat, and Zhora sat in front. All was well;
they would get back safely.

They won't take me to court; they're not the sort. They'll keep
Alyosha away from me. They will surround him with
attention. The ones who will cherish him longest of all will be
Andrei the Stool-Pigeon and his childless wife. Tanya will take
Alyosha to the seaside in summer. The Kolya who carried Alyosha
in his arms is not the Kolya who punched a seven-year-old in the
face because he had pissed himself. Marisha will love and pity little
Alyosha, with his rotten teeth and his total lack of any talent. And
Zhora, who is going to be rich, will help him generously and, who
knows, will see to it that Alyosha gets a place at university. Serge is a
different matter; he is a man with little romance in his soul; he is dry,
cynical and mistrustful. But he will end up by living with the only
person he has ever really loved—his daughter Sonya. It will all
cause dissension in our little circle, and it will keep their tongues
busy, not now but in eight years' time, and in that time Alyosha will
succeed in building up his strength, his brains and everything he
needs. I'm a clever woman; I understand these things.

Translated from the Russian by Michael Glenny.

INKA RUKA
THOSE FROM MY VILLAGE

First published in *Die Zeitgenössische Photographia in der Sowjetunion*. Edition Stemmle. Schaffhausen.

GRANTA

THE STATE OF EUROPE: CHRISTMAS EVE 1989

On 1 December 1989, *Granta* asked a number of writers how they understood the events in Central and Eastern Europe. Change had come at an incomprehensible speed: the re-burying of Imre Nagy in Hungary, the opening of the borders there, the elections in Poland, the trains of immigrants into Germany, the resignation of Erich Honecker. It seemed impossible that change could come any faster, but it did, and in November events seemed to accelerate: on 9 November, the Berlin Wall; sixteen days later, the resignation of Ladislav Adamec, the Czechoslovak prime minister. So many things in Europe would never, could never, be the same. Was it possible to record this particular moment, poised, as we felt we were at the beginning of December, between two histories: the one that existed before 9 November, and that other one, still to be defined, already being debated, which we knew we were then entering?

This is what we asked of our writers. But, even in this, our judgement of the moment was premature. By the time the fifteen writers had received our letter (the weekend, it turned out, that Gorbachev and Bush were meeting in the Mediterranean), Erich Honecker was placed under house arrest; and by the time we received their answers Gustav Husák had resigned in Czechoslovakia. The week before Christmas, the last contribution to our forum arrived; it was written by the Romanian poet Mircea Dinescu, but it could not have been mailed by him. Since May, he has been under house arrest, under the surveillance, it is reported, of eighteen security officers. The day we received his translation, we also received the first reports from Timosoara in Romania. There were no Western journalists there; we have only unconfirmed reports of indiscriminate killings—the number of deaths being mentioned is terrible to contemplate. Dinescu's contribution—what should it be called? an essay? a polemic? a cry for help?—is a reminder of the utter and insistent and implacable seriousness of the issues underlying this debate.

Josef Škvorecký

These are days of understandable, and I hope not premature, jubilation in Czechoslovakia. The generation of twenty-year-olds who were bloodied by the police and went on to topple the power monopoly of the Communist Party, are experiencing pure bliss untainted by any—even tiny—drops of sadness. That's how it should be because it's natural. The twenty-year-olds have lost nothing yet, and only conditions of extreme severity can deprive a person of the happiness, eagerness and excitement that is youth. Difficulties, harassments, attempts to curb their freedom appear to young people as adventures, of which the regime has provided them with plenty, particularly in its lunatic campaigns against their favourite music. In these crusades the youngsters turned victorious, years before the present triumph. Nothing mars their euphoria now.

As one turns to the generation of their parents, now in their early forties, the picture changes. Two decades ago, when they were twenty themselves, this generation was as euphoric as their sons and daughters are today. But the Big Lie descended on Czechoslovakia and those who were starting adult life in 1968 lost their most creative, and potentially happiest, years to the abomination called *Realsozialismus*. There is sadness in their elation, but they still have a good reason to rejoice: at forty, one may still begin anew, and almost half of life lies ahead.

For the grandmothers and grandfathers, now in their sixties, the sadness changes to bitterness. They are the generation of the uranium mines, of the show trials, of the petty chicanery of security screenings; the closely watched generation for whom admission to universities was determined not by talent but by political reliability. Too many were never able to achieve what, at twenty, when life was hope and eagerness, they had thought they would. At sixty it's too late.

Of course everybody is glad that the bell tolls for the oppressive regimes that have been deforming human lives in Czechoslovakia since 1939—if this is indeed their definitive end. But those who have lived there cannot be blissfully unaware of what happened on

127

the totalitarian 'road to socialism'. That road is literally paved with human skulls. Where did it lead? To the social security of the jail? In many lands it led not even to that, but rather to a society resembling a concentration camp.

It all appears to be a huge joke played on mankind by history. The joke, however, is ebony black.

The days of the totalitarians may be numbered in most of Europe. Elsewhere they evidently are not; in some places they are just beginning. At universities in the West professors still preach the theory which was the backbone of the longer-lasting of the two deadening social experiments in our century. But Marx was right on one point: the only criterion of a theory's validity is the test of practice.

Let us rejoice by all means. I don't want to spoil the celebration. It's just that I've never been good at euphoria and I cannot purge my mind of some thoughts.

Sorry.

George Steiner

I am writing this note on 5 December 1989. It may be absurdly dated by the time it appears.

This is the obvious point. The speed of events in Eastern Europe, the hectic complexities of inward collapse and realignment are such as to make the morning papers obsolete before evening. There may have been comparable *accelarandos* before this: in France, from June to September 1789 (there is a haunting leap from that date to ours); or during those 'ten days that shook the world' in Lenin's Petrograd. But the geographical scale of the current earthquake, its ideological and ethnic diversity, the planetary interests which are implicated, do make it almost impossible to respond sensibly, let alone have any worthwhile foresight.

A touch of exultant irony is allowed in the face, precisely, of this triumph of the unexpected. No economist-pundit, no geopolitical strategist, no 'Kremlinologist' or socio-economic analyst foresaw what we are living through. There was, indeed, all manner of speculation on the decay of institutions and distributive means in the Soviet Union. Some sort of challenge in Poland was on the cards. But all the pretentious jargon, the econometric projection-charts, the formalistic studies of international relations, have proved fatuous. We are back with Plutarch. The apocalypse of hope has been started by one man.

Historians will generate volumes of hindsight, sociologists and economists will juggle determinants and predictable certainties. Eyewash. The fact is that we know next to nothing of the intuitive panic, the alarmed vision, the gambler's stab into the unknown which may or may not have brought on Gorbachev's hoisting of the old, sclerotic but certainly defensible order. If Plutarch won't do, we are back to the miraculous, to the tears of the Black Virgin over Poland, to the incensed saints and patriarchs who have taken to heart the long strangulation of Hungary, of Bulgaria. We are back to the enigmatic pulse-beat of the messianic.

Second gloss: the cardinal ambiguity in the role of the United States. That role is now almost surrealistically irrelevant. Bush bobbing on the waves of Malta is an apt picture. The US appears to be becoming a provincial colossus, ignorant of, indifferent towards Europe. It will have its heavy hands full with Latin and Central America, with the derisive patronage of Japan. Europe is again on its own.

On the other hand, the image, the 'symbol-news' of America has been decisive. The millions who poured westward through the broken Berlin Wall, the young of Budapest, Sofia, Prague or Moscow, are not inebriate with some abstract passion for freedom, for social justice, for the flowering of culture. It is a TV-revolution we are witnessing, a rush towards the 'California-promise' that America has offered to the common man on this tired earth. American standards of dress, nourishment, locomotion, entertainment, housing are today the concrete utopia in revolutions. With *Dallas* being viewed east of the Wall, the dismemberment of the regime may have become inevitable. Video-cassettes, porno-cassettes, American-style cosmetics and fast foods, not editions of Mill, de Tocqueville or Solzhenitsyn, were the prizes snatched from every West Berlin shelf by the liberated. The new temples to liberty (the 1789 dream) will be McDonald's and Kentucky Fried Chicken.

Hence the paradox: as the US declines into its own 'pursuit of happiness', the packaged promise, the bright after-glow of that pursuit becomes essential in Eastern Europe and, very probably, in the post-medieval, Asiatic morass of the Soviet Union.

Everything can still go wrong. Gorbachev's survival seems to hang by a thread. Clearly, the old guard on the right is desperate, the new radicals on the left are crazily impatient. Slovak indifference chills the new Prague Spring. Can the lunatic and sadistic self-destruction of Romania be halted? What will happen if Yugoslavia splits? Not only in Peking are there large squares ideal for tanks. One prays and hopes and rejoices and rages at the tepid bureaucracies of the Common Market and the prim neo-isolationism of Thatcherite Britain. Everywhere, we are witnessing an almost mad race between resurgent nationalism, ethnic hatreds and the counter-force of potential prosperity and free exchange.

The variant on Judaic-messianic idealism, on the prophetic

vision of a kingdom of justice on earth, which we call Marxism, brought intolerable bestiality, suffering and practical failure to hundreds of millions of men and women. The lifting of that yoke is cause for utter gratitude and relief. But the source of the hideous misprision is not ignoble (as was that of Nazi racism): it lies in a terrible over-estimate of man's capacities for altruism, for purity, for intellectual-philosophic sustenance. The theatres in East Berlin performed the classics when heavy metal and American musicals were wanted. The bookstores displayed Lessing and Goethe and Tolstoy, but Archer and Collins were dreamed of. The present collapse of Marxist-Leninist despotisms marks the vengeful termination of a compliment to man—probably illusory—but positive none the less.

What will step into the turbulent vacuum? Fundamentalist religion is clawing at our doors. And money shouts at us. The West inhabits a money-crazed amusement-arcade. The scientific-technological pin-ball machines ring and glitter brilliantly. But the imperatives of privacy, of autonomous imagining, of tact and spirit and scruple in the face of non-utilitarian values, are dimmed. And we lay waste the natural world. Only an autistic mandarin would deny to the mass of his fellow men and women the improved living-standards, the bread and circuses they are now fighting, emigrating or dreaming towards. But if one is possessed of the cancer of thought, of art, of utopian speculation, the shadows at the heart of the carnival are equally present.

The knout on the one hand; the cheeseburger on the other. The Gulag of the old East, the insertion of panty-hose ads between gas-oven sequences of *Holocaust* on TV in the new West. That alternative *must* be proved false if man is to be man. Will the breaking of the walls make the choices more fruitful and meaningful, more attuned to human potential and limitation? Only a fool would prophesy.

P.S. 11 December. Events have in fact, accelerated during the past six days. The Prague secret police are now headed by a man who was their prisoner less than four weeks ago. There is no East German government. Bulgaria is swinging towards a multi-party scheme. The Baltic republics are defying Moscow.

I can make more precise the notion of the Marxist overestimate of man. It was Moses's error all over again (remember his desperate rages and death short of the promised land), and Christ's illusion. As that error, and its savage cost, are once again made plain and amended, will Jew-hatred, in the persistent eschatological sense, smoulder into heat? Already there are ugly signals from Hungary and East Germany.

Jurek Becker

'Really existing socialism' is on the way out, no question. Good thing too, if you fix your mind on the true condition of life in the socialist states, and not the fictional version which their leaders have passed off as the truth. The West has won—and there's the rub.

Here in the West, we live in societies that have no particular goal or objective. If there is any guiding principle, it's consumerism. In theory, we can increase our consumption until the planet lies about us in ruins and, given current trends, that's precisely what will happen. In spite of everything we knew and understood about them, we had a hope that the socialist states might find a different path. That hope is gone. People there are desperate to adopt the principles of the West: the conversion of as many goods as possible into rubbish (which is what consumption means), and the free expression of all types of ideas (accompanied by a growing reluctance to think at all). Converts are liable to be especially strict and zealous in the observance of their new faith; I expect the same will apply to the people of these recently converted nations.

A few days ago, I was talking to a friend about the possibility of German reunification, the conversation that all Germans have been having these past days and weeks. He was in favour of it, I was against. After a while he lost his temper with me, and asked me how I could possibly justify the continued existence of the German Democratic Republic. I started thinking, and I'm still thinking now. If I can't think of any reasons, I shall have to change my mind and become a supporter of reunification. I shall have to be in favour of turning Eastern Europe into an extension of Western Europe.

The only argument I am able to come up with is perhaps more suitable for a poem than a political discussion: the most important thing about socialist states isn't any tangible achievements, but the fact that they give us a chance. Things are not cut and dried as they are here. The uncertainty there doesn't promise anything, of course, but it's our only hope for the continued existence of humanity. Eastern Europe looks to me like one last attempt. And when it's over, it'll be time to withdraw our money from the bank, and start hitting the bottle in earnest.

Translated from the German by Michael Hofmann

Building the Berlin Wall, 1961.

Hans Magnus Enzensberger

You find them in every European capital, in the centre of the city, where space is symbolic: corpulent centaurs, metal hermaphrodites, Roman emperors, Grand Dukes, eternally victorious generals. Under their hoofs, civil servants hurry to their ministries, or spectators into the opera, or believers to Mass. They represent the European hero, without whom the history of the continent is barely imaginable. But with the invention of the motor car, the spirit of the age dismounted—Lenin and Mussolini, Franco and Stalin, all managed without a whinnying undercarriage and the stockpiles of heroes in stone were shipped off to Caribbean islands or Siberian combines. Inflation and elephantiasis heralded the end of the hero whose principal preoccupations were conquest, triumph and delusions of grandeur.

Writers saw it coming. A hundred years ago literature waved goodbye to those larger-than-life characters whose very creation it had helped bring about. The victory song and the tales of derring-do belong now to prehistory. No one is interested in Augustus or Alexander; it is Bouvard and Pecuchet or Vladimir and Estragon. Frederick the Great and Napoleon have been relegated to the literary basement; as for those Hymns to Hitler and Odes to Stalin—they were destined for the scrapheap from the very start.

In the past few decades, a more significant protagonist has stepped forward: a hero of a new kind, representing not victory, conquest and triumph, but renunciation, reduction and dismantling. We have every reason to concern ourselves with these specialists in denial, for our continent depends on them if it is to survive.

It was Clausewitz, the doyen of strategic thinking, who showed that retreat is the most difficult of all operations. That applies in politics as well. The *non plus ultra* in the art of the possible consists of withdrawing from an untenable position. But if the stature of the hero is proportional to the difficulty of the task before him, then it follows that our concept of the heroic needs not only to be revised, but to be stood on its head. Any cretin can throw a bomb. It is a thousand times more difficult to defuse one.

Popular opinion, especially in Germany, holds to the traditional view. It demands steadfastness of purpose, insisting on a political morality which places single-mindedness and adherence to principle above all else, even, if it comes to it, above respect for human life. This unambiguity is not on offer from the heroes of retreat. Retreating from a position you have held involves not only surrendering the middle ground, but also giving up a part of yourself. Such a move cannot succeed without a separation of character and role. The expert dismantler shows his political mettle by taking this ambiguity on to himself.

The paradigm is particularly apparent in the wake of this century's totalitarian dictatorships. At first the significance of the pioneers of retreat was barely detectable. People still claim that Nikita Khrushchev didn't know what he was doing, that he couldn't have guessed the implications of his actions; after all, he talked of perfecting communism, not of abolishing it. And yet, in his famous speech to the Twentieth Party Congress, he sowed more than the seeds of his own downfall. His intellectual horizons may have been narrow; his strategy clumsy and his manner arrogant, but he showed more courage in his own beliefs than almost any other politician of his generation. It was precisely the unsteady side to his character that suited him for his task. Today the subversive logic of his credentials as a hero lie open for all to see: the deconstruction of the Soviet empire began with him.

The internal contradictions of the historical demolition man were more starkly exposed in the career of János Kádár. This man who, a few months ago, was buried quietly and unobtrusively in Budapest, made a pact with the occupying forces after the failed uprising of 1956. It is rumoured that he was responsible for 800 death sentences. Hardly had the victims of his repression been buried than he got to work on the task that was to occupy him for the next thirty years: the patient undermining of the absolute dictatorship of the Communist Party. It is surprising that there was no serious disturbance; there were constant set-backs and shattered hopes, but through compromise and tactical manoeuvring Kádár's process moved inexorably forward. Without the Hungarian precedent it is hard to see how the dissolution of the Eastern Bloc would have begun; Kádár's trail-blazing role in this is beyond dispute. It is equally clear that he was no match for the forces he helped to unleash. His was the archetypal fate of the historical demolition man: in doing his job he ended up undermining his own position. The dynamic he set in motion hurled him aside, and he was buried by his own successes.

Adolfo Suarez, General Secretary of the Spanish phalange, became prime minister after Franco's death. In a meticulously planned coup he did away with the regime, installed his own Unity Party in power and forced through a democratic constitution; the operation was delicate and dangerous. This was no vague hunch, like Khrushchev's; this was the work of an intelligence at the height of its awareness: a military putsch would have led to bloody repression and perhaps a new civil war.

This course of action again is inconceivable from someone unable to differentiate beyond black sheep and white sheep. Suarez played a role in and gained advantage from the Franco regime. Had he not belonged to the innermost circles of power he would not have been in a position to abolish the dictatorship. At the same time, his past earned him the undying mistrust of all democrats. Indeed, Spain has not forgiven him to this day. In the eyes of his former comrades he was a traitor; those whose path he had cleared saw him as an opportunist. After abdicating his leading role in the period of transition he never found his feet again. His role in the party system of the republic has remained obscure. The hero of retreat can only be sure of one thing: the ingratitude of the fatherland.

The moral dilemma assumes almost tragic dimensions in the figure of Wojciech Jaruzelski. In 1981, he saved Poland from the inevitability of Soviet invasion. The price of salvation was the introduction of martial law and the internment of those very members of the unofficial opposition who today run the country under his presidency. The resounding success of his policies did not spare him the wrath of the Polish people, a large number of whom regard him to this day with utter hatred. No one cheers him; he will never escape the ghost of his past actions. Yet his moral strength lies in the fact that he knew from the very beginning that this is how it would turn out. No one has ever seen him smile. With his stiff, lifeless gestures and his eyes hidden behind dark

Nikita Khruschev, September, 1960.

sunglasses he personifies the patriot as martyr. This political Saint Sebastian is a figure of Shakespearean stature.

The same cannot be said of those who lagged behind him. Egon Krenz and Ladislav Adamec will in all probability merit only a footnote in history, the one as a burlesque, the other a petty bourgeois version of the heroic rearguard. But neither the grin of the German nor the fatherly countenance of the Czech should be allowed to obscure the importance of the part they played. The very agility we reproach them for has been their only service. In that paralysing stillness of the pregnant moment, when one side waits for the other to move and nothing happens, someone had to be the first to clear his throat, to utter the first half-choked whisper that started the avalanche. 'Someone', a German social democrat once said, 'has to be the bloodhound.' Seventy years later someone had to spike the bloodhounds' guns, although as it turned out it was a communist Pulcinella who broke the deadly silence. No one will cherish his memory. This in itself makes him memorable.

The real hero of deconstruction, however, is himself the driving force. Mikhail Gorbachev is the initiator of a process with which other, willingly or unwillingly, can only struggle to keep up. His is—of this we can probably now be certain—a timeless figure. The sheer size of the task he has taken on is without precedent. He is attempting to dismantle the second to the last remaining monolithic empire of the twentieth century without the use of force, without panic, in peace. Whether he can succeed remains to be seen; he has already achieved what no one, even a few months ago, would have believed possible. It took long enough before the rest of the world began to understand what he was doing. The superior intelligence, the moral boldness, the far-reaching perspective of the man lay so far outside the horizons of the political élite, east and west, that no government dared take him at his word.

Gorbachev has no illusions about his popularity at home. The greatest proponent of the politics of doing without is confronted at every step with demands for something *positive*, as if it were enough simply to promise the people another golden future where

General Wojciech Jaruzelski, December 1982.

everyone would receive free soap, rockets and brotherly affection, each according to his needs; as if there were any other way forward but by retreating; as if there were any other hope for the future but by disarming the Leviathan and searching for a way out of the nightmare and back to normality. It goes without saying that the protagonist risks his life with every step he takes on this path. He is surrounded on the right and on the left by enemies old and new, loud and silent. As befits the hero, Mikhail Gorbachev is a very lonely man.

Not that we should lionize these greater and lesser heroes of deconstruction; they are not asking for that. Any memorial would be superfluous. It is time, however, to take them seriously, to look more closely at what they have in common and how they differ. A political morality which recognizes only good and evil spirits will not be up to this task.

A German philosopher once said that by the end of the century the question would no longer be one of improving the world but of saving it, which applies not only to those dictatorships whose elaborate dismantling we have watched with our own eyes. The Western democracies are also facing an unprecedented dissolution. The military aspect is only one of many. We must also withdraw from our untenable position in the war of debt against the Third World, and the most difficult retreat of all will be in the war against the biosphere which we have been waging since the industrial revolution. It is time for our own diminutive statesmen to measure up to the demolition experts. An energy or transport policy worthy of the name will only come about through a strategic retreat. Certain large industries—ultimately no less threatening than one-party rule—will have to be broken up. The courage and conviction necessary to bring this about will hardly be greater than those the communist functionary had to summon up to do away with his party's monopoly.

But instead our political leadership senses victory, indulging in ridiculous posturing and self-satisfied lies. It gloats and it stonewalls, thinking it can master the future by sitting it out. It hasn't the slightest idea about the moral imperative of sacrifice. It knows nothing of the politics of retreat. It has a lot to learn.

Translated from the German by Piers Spence

Werner Krätschell

I think of three moments.

The first is on a Sunday, 13 August 1961: Lake Mälar in
Sweden. One of the best summers of my life. I am in Finland with
Albert, my favourite among eight brothers and sisters—he is
twenty and I am twenty-one. We have left our parents' home in
East Berlin and have set out 'illegally': we didn't get permission for
our journey and so have committed a criminal offence. We flew
from West Berlin to Hamburg, where we got West German
passports, and continued our journey northwards, to the land of
our dreams, as citizens of the Federal Republic.

Monday, 14 August 1961: The very next day the manager of the
estate where we're staying comes rushing into the kitchen. We are
eating breakfast, and he is shouting: 'It's all over, boys. You can't
go back again. They've closed the borders.' He shows us the
newspapers and the photos are upsetting.

In the evening we sit by the stove in our little guest house. It is
built out over the lake and was once used by the washer women for
their hard work. We have a decision to make. Albert wants to stay.
He is about to get his school diploma in West Berlin. I want to go
back. I am studying theology and don't want to stop. Following an
old family tradition, I want to become a minister, a minister 'in the
East'. Every generation of our family has had one: I want to return
to the parsonage, where, apart from my youngest sister, only my
parents now remain. Mother has multiple sclerosis. That, too, is a
reason.

9 November 1989: In the evening, in the historic Friedrichstadt
French church, I preside over one of the many recent and
remarkable political meetings. I am joined by Manfred Stolpe, one
of the leaders of the Protestant Church, and Lothar de Maizière,
who, tomorrow, will be elected chairman of the Christian
Democrats. All the guilty political parties have sent representatives
to our meeting; we are witnessing a palace revolt amid members of
this previously colourless, cowardly, corrupt Party. The

Communist, Professor Döhle, speaks first. There is—because of the poor acoustics—laughter and spontaneous applause as I lead him to the front. For the first time in his life he now stands—irritated but happy—in a pulpit, with ecclesiastical permission, in the middle of the camp of the old 'class enemy', the Church. What an image, what emotion! Is it a foretaste of the night to come?

On leaving the church, a French journalist tells me a strange piece of news: Schabowski, the Communist Party boss in Berlin, and Egon Krenz, have hinted at the possibility that the border might be opened. I waste no time and drive quickly to Pankow. As I pass the Gethsemane church on Schönhauser Allee, I see images of the violence that occurred at the beginning of last month: once again, I see the police, the army, the 'Stasi' men, the armoured vehicles and shadowy figures wielding batons. I reach our home and find Konstanze, my twenty-year-old daughter and her friend Astrid, who is twenty-one. Rapidly we jump into the car and drive at great speed to the nearest border crossing: Bornholmer Strasse.

Dream and reality become confused. The guards let us through: the girls cry. They cling together tightly on the back seat, as if they're expecting an air raid. We are crossing the strip that for twenty-eight years has been a death zone. And suddenly we see West Berliners. They wave, cheer, shout. I drive down Osloer Strasse to my old school where I got my diploma in 1960. We don't stay long, however, and must return right away because there are still two younger children sleeping at home, and because Astrid is pregnant, and because I have to fly to London early in the morning. But, when we turn around, we see that we are not going to get through. We were among the very first to cross the border. Now the news has spread like wild fire. Hundreds, thousands block our way. There are people who recognize me and they pull open the car door: kisses and tears and we are all in a trance. Astrid, suddenly, tells me to stop the car at the next intersection. She wants only to put her foot down on the street just once. Touching the ground. Armstrong after the moon landing. She has never been in the West before.

All around us, people are beating their fists on my car with joy. The dents will remain, souvenirs of that night.

I hardly sleep and in the morning pass 'normally' through the

Raymond Depardon (Magnum)

Children's game, Berlin 1961.

Friedrichstrasse crossing point. Hundreds crowd through the narrow doors, which were, until yesterday, the 'gates of inhumanity'. My son Joachim stands on the other side. His 'summer at Lake Mälar' was in Hungary and was called 'Balaton'. There, also in August, he made his decision to leave his country and his parents' home. He was without hope. In May and June, he had demonstrated against both the rigging of the elections that had taken place earlier this year and the bloody suppression of the popular movement in China. The consequences were unpleasant. He attempted to escape, and, on his first attempt, he was caught by the Hungarian soldiers. He tried again, and, on his second attempt, he ran for his life. Now he's here. Weeks of pain—for him and for us—are over. His brother Johannes (thirteen) and sister Karoline (seven) don't yet understand the new possibilities. In August Joachim was still twenty-one. His decision was different from mine. Or was it just the same?

The twenty-eight years between: Not until I am on the plane on my way to London and I am alone, alone for the first time after all these dramatic weeks. What have these twenty-eight years meant to you?

Back then, at Lake Mälar in Sweden, I could not imagine that I would one day be married or that I would one day have children. Have they suffered? Yes: there have been hardships; no: there has been inner wealth. They grew up in a parsonage, where the beggar was as welcome as the diplomat, the worker as welcome as the poet. They have had music and Christmas, the landscape of the Mark Brandenburg and good friends. The friends came from the East and West and brought reports and thoughts which saved us from being provincial. And conversation: dense and full of passion. The way we were in those conversations, that's how we really were.

We lived in that other world made wretched by the Communists. We have known the broken and the damned and the ones deprived of their citizen rights. I am only realizing now how, for twenty-eight years, I got caught up again and again by their stories and by the need, therefore, to help them. So many times it had been necessary to get people 'to the West'—very often by difficult routes. They didn't want to live here, or they couldn't live here, or they weren't allowed to live here any more—it was always a question of life. But it was also necessary to protect the people who wanted or had to stay here, and who had fought back against the system of repression with their own small strength. I think of the groups that gathered in our churches and community centres since the beginning of the eighties, made up of people who were discovering, without knowing it, the principle of non-violence, who were discovering as well that it was a political instrument, one that they then developed in themselves and for others, so that it became the hallmark of the changes.

What I can hear now, here and from the movements in Eastern Europe, is not only a cry for freedom and human dignity; I also hear an urgent plea to the community of Western Europe not to forget us. We want to be part of things when, in 1992, the Western European Community, makes the leap into a better life. We don't want to become Europe's 'Third World'. I desire an end to the German as well as to the European division, in which the human dignity of the East Germans and the East Europeans is not damaged, but strengthened.

Translated from the German by Martin Chalmers

Isaiah Berlin

You ask me for a response to the events in Europe. I have nothing
new to say: my reactions are similar to those of virtually everyone I
know, or know of—astonishment, exhilaration, happiness. When
men and women imprisoned for a long time by oppressive and
brutal regimes are able to break free, at any rate from some of their
chains, and after many years know even the beginnings of genuine
freedom, how can anyone with the smallest spark of human feeling
not be profoundly moved? One can only add, as Madame
Bonaparte said when congratulated on the historically unique
distinction of being mother to an emperor, three kings and a queen,
'*Oui, pourvu que ça dure.*' If only we could be sure that there will
not be a relapse, particularly in the Soviet Union, as some
observers fear.

The obvious parallel, which must have struck everyone, is the
similarity of these events to the revolutions of 1848–49, when a
great upsurge of liberal and democratic feeling toppled
governments in Paris, Rome, Venice, Berlin, Dresden, Vienna,
Budapest. The late Sir Lewis Namier attributed the failure of these
revolutions—for by 1850 they were all dead—to their having been,
in his words, 'a Revolution of Intellectuals'. However this may be,
we also know that it was the forces unleashed against these
revolutions—the armies of Prussia and Austria-Hungary, the
southern Slav battalions, the agents of Napoleon III in France and
Italy, and, above all, the Czar's troops in Budapest—that crushed
this movement and restored something like the *status quo*.
Fortunately, the situation today does not look similar. The current
movements have developed into genuine, spontaneous popular
risings, which plainly embrace all classes. We can remain
optimistic.

Apart from these general reflections, there is a particular thing
which has struck me forcibly—the survival, against all odds, of the
Russian intelligentsia. An intelligentsia is not identical with
intellectuals. Intellectuals are persons who, as someone said,
simply want ideas to be as interesting as possible. Intelligentsia,
however, is a Russian word and a Russian phenomenon. Born in

the second quarter of the nineteenth century, it was a movement of educated, morally sensitive Russians stirred to indignation by an obscurantist Church; by a brutally oppressive state indifferent to the squalor, poverty and illiteracy in which the great majority of the population lived; by a governing class which they saw as trampling on human rights and impeding moral and intellectual progress. They believed in personal and political liberty, in the removal of irrational social inequalities and in truth, which they identified to some degree with scientific progress. They held a view of enlightenment that they associated with Western liberalism and democracy.

The intelligentsia, for the most part, consisted of members of the professions. The best known were the writers—all the great names (even Dostoyevsky in his younger days) were in various degrees and fashions engaged in the fight for freedom. It was the descendants of these people who were largely responsible for making the February Revolution of 1917. Some of its members who believed in extreme measures took part in the suppression of this revolution and the establishment of Soviet communism in Russia, and later elsewhere. In due course the intelligentsia was by degrees systematically destroyed, but it did not wholly perish.

When I was in the Soviet Union in 1945, I met not only two great poets and their friends and allies who had grown to maturity before the Revolution, but also younger people, mostly children or grandchildren of academics, librarians, museum-keepers, translators and other members of the old intelligentsia, who had managed to survive in obscure corners of Soviet society. But there seemed to be not many of them left. There was, of course, a term 'Soviet intelligentsia', often used in state publications, and meaning members of the professions. But there was little evidence that this term was much more than a homonym, that they were in fact heirs of the intelligentsia in the older sense, men and women who pursued the ideals which I have mentioned. My impression was that what remained of the true intelligentsia was dying.

In the course of the last two years, I have discovered, to my great surprise and delight, that I was mistaken. I have met Soviet citizens, comparatively young, and clearly representative of a large number of similar people, who seemed to have retained the moral character, the intellectual integrity, the sensitive imagination and immense human attractiveness of the old intelligentsia. They are to be found mainly among writers, musicians, painters, artists in many spheres—the theatre and cinema—and, of course, among academics. The most famous among them, Andrey Dimitrievich Sakharov, would have been perfectly at home in the world of Turgenev, Herzen, Belinsky, Saltykov, Annenkov and their friends in the 1840s and 50s. Sakharov, whose untimely end I mourn as deeply as anyone, seems to me to belong heart and soul to this noble tradition. His scientific outlook, unbelievable courage, physical and moral, above all his unswerving dedication to truth, makes it impossible not to see him as the ideal representative, in our time, of all that was most pure-hearted and humane in the members of the intelligentsia, old and new. Moreover, like them, and I speak from personal acquaintance, he was civilized to his fingertips and possessed what I can only call great moral charm. His vigorous intellect and lively interest in books, ideas, people, political issues seemed to me, tired as he was, to have survived his terrible maltreatment. Nor was he alone. The survival of the entire culture to which he belonged underneath the ashes and rubble of dreadful historical experience appears to me a miraculous fact. Surely this gives grounds for optimism. What is true of Russia may be even more true of the other peoples who are throwing off their shackles—where the oppressors have been in power for a shorter period and where civilized values and memories of past freedom are a living force in the still unexhausted survivors of an earlier time.

The study of the ideas and activities of the nineteenth-century Russian intelligentsia has occupied me for some years, and to find that, so far from being buried in the past, this movement—as it is still right to call it—has survived and is regaining its health and freedom, is a revelation and a source of great delight to me. The Russians are a great people, their creative powers are immense, and, once set free, there is no telling what they may give to the world. A new barbarism is always possible, but I see little prospect of it at present. That evils can, after all, be conquered, that the end of enslavement is in progress, are things of which men can be reasonably proud.

Andrei Sinyavsky

Many of our friends from the Soviet Union come to visit us in Paris—Soviet writers, artists and journalists—and I ask all of them: 'Who is running the country? And what's going to happen tomorrow?' For a long time now I have been getting the same answer: 'We don't know!'

Just think: this was my country, where for decades nothing happened, where one day was exactly like another, and you could predict the future years and kilometres ahead (turn to the right, and you join the Communist Party, eventually becoming one of the bosses; turn to the left, and they call you a dissident and put you in prison). Suddenly the country doesn't know what will happen next week. Nobody in the world knows.

We, the Russians, are once more in the vanguard, once more the most interesting phenomenon on earth—I would even say as an *artistic* phenomenon: like a novel whose ending none of us knows.

Little was needed to make this happen. First the people were granted a relative freedom of speech. Second the idea of global communism, for the sake of which so many pointless sacrifices had been made, was abolished (or at least forgotten for a while). And the very soil, as a result, proved to be immediately fruitful.

But it is here, too, that we find new dangers growing within the empire at its moment of transformation: the dangers of xenophobia and ethnic conflict. In particular, to judge from the press, I see a new form of Russian nazism gathering strength. I see the seeds of it, for instance, in a work recently published in Moscow by Igor Shafarevich entitled *Russophobia*, in which, developing one of Solzhenitsyn's ideas, the author builds up the myth of the Jews as the original and principal enemy of the Russian people. Igor Shafarevich is a world-class mathematician, a member of the Soviet Academy of Sciences, an honorary member or professor of several European academies and universities. Yet the argument of his book coincides with the theoreticians of German Nazism, from Hitler to Rosenberg (perhaps the coincidence is unconscious, but there are passages which seem like verbatim allusions). The thesis is couched in measured, reflective, academic terms. It can be summarized

151

thus: a small people, that is the Jews, (the Russophobes of the titles), is waging a centuries-old battle to the death against a large nation (in this case Russia): 'Russophobe literature is strongly influenced by Jewish nationalist sentiments,' he writes. Among the Russophobes he numbers Galich and Vysotsky, Korzhavin and Amalrik, Grossman and Tarkovsky, Ilf and Petrov, Byalik and Babel. In the past, 'the typical representative of this tendency [in this particular instance an anti-German one] was Heine.' Similar efforts at domination by representatives of this small nation are found, he explains, in 'the influence of Freud as a thinker, the fame of the composer Schönberg, the artist Picasso, the writer Kafka or the poet Brodsky.' The aim of this small nation, writes Shafarevich in conclusion, is the ultimate destruction of the religious and national foundations of our life, and at the same time, given the first opportunity, the ruthlessly purposive subversion of our national destiny, resulting in a new and terminal catastrophe, after which probably nothing will be left of our [i.e. the Russian] people.'

I am by no means against the publication of Shafarevich's *Russophobia*, especially in Russia, after so many years of being deprived of the freedom of expression. But I am worried by the silence surrounding the appearance of this book, the absence of any serious discussion of it. The danger of the game Shafarevich is playing lies not so much in his ideas, which are trivial enough, as in the soil on which they are falling.

Anti-Semitic ideas have been taken up in the Soviet Union by both the mob and intellectuals. Two events took place recently in Moscow: an anti-Semitic demonstration by the society known as *Pamyat* ('Memory'), which was held in Red Square (and therefore had official permission from the authorities), and an anti-Semitic plenary session of the Union of Writers of the Russian Federation. The demonstration of the mob ended with it singing a song whose opening lines are:

Arise, thou mighty nation,
Arise, take up the sword!
Against the Yids' foul domination,
Against that cursed horde

The speakers at the plenary meeting of Russian intellectuals included the distinguished novelists Valentin Rasputin and Vassily Bielov. Rasputin accompanied Gorbachev on his visit to China; Bielov went with him to Finland. The meeting ended with the editor of the literary journal *October* being dismissed for publishing works described as 'anti-patriotic and Russophobe'.

Nationalism in itself is not a serious threat—it can, on occasion, actually be of value to a nation—until it starts to produce, without any substantive grounds, that venomous by-product: 'the enemy'. In the past, the Soviet Union had the 'class enemy'. The struggle against the class enemy grew more and more intense just as all classes were being liquidated until indeed there were no more classes left. And now the Russian nationalists, who call themselves 'patriots', have summoned up 'Russophobia', a modification of the Leninist-Stalinist idea of 'bourgeois encirclement' and 'bourgeois penetration'. The 'Russophobe' is a variant of those terrible Stalinist inventions 'enemy of the people' and 'ideological saboteur'.

All of them are, of course, myths.

But the definition of 'Russophobia' has expanded to threatening dimensions. It incorporates the 'soul-less' West, poisoned through and through by pornography and drug addiction and longing only to destroy the Russian people, who are the incarnation of mankind's conscience. Then there are the enemies within—the liberals and democrats, the intellectuals, the black-market operators, the dissidents and the Jews. Both the old-style myth of the bourgeois threat and the new version—Russophobia—I find equally repellent, not only for their vulgarity but for the very dangerous undertone of hatred which they contain. After all, if Russia's ills and misfortunes derive from its Western Russophobe enemies and its internal Russophobe enemies, and these enemies want to destroy the soul, the body and the memory of the nation, of Russian culture and of the entire Russian people, why not put an end to all these 'parasites', 'cosmopolitans' and 'pluralists' at a stroke?

When a multi-national empire disintegrates, or finds itself on the verge of falling apart, the peoples who constitute it develop various forms of nationalism. This has marked the break-up of many great empires. A powerful, militant Russian nationalism is arising to shore up and protect the Soviet Empire. As I see it from here, the Soviet Union at the moment is like a garage full of cans of petrol which are giving off so much vapour that the place is ready to explode. In that volatile atmosphere, the Russian nationalists are playing with matches, and one of the most inflammatory matches is called 'Russophobia'.

Why do they play with these matches? To bring about a national religious revival? God preserve us from any such thing! And may Christ forgive us for once again linking His name with the urge to launch massacres and pogroms.

Translated from the Russian by Michael Glenny

Abraham Brumberg

My grandfather, a prosperous merchant equally at home among cosmopolitan financiers and in the insular world of his native Lithuanian *shtetl*, lived and died in History. In 1918, he was stood up against a wall and shot, together with two of his sons, by Red Army conscripts. It was merely a chance historical moment that made my grandfather and his sons victims of the Bolshevik Revolution rather than of its enemies—or of local anti-Semitic cutthroats. But it cast a long shadow.

My father, a free-thinking socialist, was forced to flee the country in 1925. He had been involved in one of those student strikes which the Polish police, not keen on ideological distinctions, regarded as yet another 'Judeo-Communist' plot. Nine years later, back in Poland as director of a children's sanatorium maintained by the Jewish socialist 'Bund', he used his revolver (the first and only time in his life) to fight off a group of communists bent on destroying this bastion of 'social fascism'. Another chance historical moment?

When the war broke out, my parents and I set off on a trek that eventually took us from Warsaw to Soviet-occupied Vilna. Since the NKVD was combing the town for socialists, liberals, 'nationalists' and other enemies of the people, my father went into hiding, leaving my mother and me with local relatives. He surfaced several weeks later, when Vilna (now Vilnius) was turned over to Lithuania, only to disappear again when Soviet troops re-occupied Lithuania and the other two Baltic states.

For obvious reasons I, at the age of twelve, turned out to be the sole hold-out in my class against the allurements of revolutionary rhetoric. All the others had joined the Red Pioneers. One day, we were reading aloud a hymn to Stalin written by Itzik Feffer, a Soviet Yiddish poet later executed as a spy. Each student was told to read one stanza. When it was my turn, I declaimed, though apparently without enough ardour:

He is deeper than the oceans,
He is higher than the peaks,
There is no one on this globe
Quite remotely like him.

Apparently, for my schoolmates, on the look out for evidence of ideological turpitude, loudly demanded that the teacher force me to 'read the stanza again—with more feeling.' The teacher, not a communist, looked sad—and complied. So did I, but the lesson sank in: terror needs no jails or bayonets to be effective.

My family managed to reach the United States in 1941. Wracked by questions, I began reading voraciously, seeking answers in works by eyewitnesses to history, erstwhile believers, anathemized enemies (for instance Leon Trotsky) and sympathetic but critical scholars such as Sidney Hook and William H. Chamberlin. I memorized entire chunks of the report by the Commission of Inquiry on the first two Moscow Trials (John Dewey, *Not Guilty*) and hurled them at my gauchist fellow students in New York's City College. We argued about the communist coups in Eastern Europe, whether Tito was a fascist beast, and whether Stalin was the 'gravedigger of the Revolution' or—in the words of Isaac Deutscher—the 'man who dragged Russia, screaming and kicking, into the twentieth century.'

And now, suddenly, there is change. In Czechoslovakia, the change was the death knell of the Communist Party, and it sounded when the workers laid down their tools on 27 November. But in East Germany, the change came the moment that popular discontent turned to fury at the disclosures of massive corruption within the red bourgeoisie. The Germans, apparently, actually believed that Honecker *et al* lived as ascetically as Vladimir Ilyich Lenin. Now they know otherwise. Will they still ask themselves how dedicated communists who had spent years in Hitler's jails and camps had turned into sanctimonious revellers? Or will they conclude that Communists had always been, *au fond*, a pack of gangsters? In Poland, that seems to be the conclusion. 'Nothing but a pack of gangsters' is now the preferred sobriquet for all communists, used indiscriminately even by Solidarity leaders whose past ties to the party were based on rather more than lust for power and privileges.

Questions: they generate more questions. Stalin was a monster, Lenin hardly a saint and Marx a prophet *manque*; but have their mistakes, misdeeds and villainies sullied the goal of a just society? Did the path chosen by Lenin and the other founders of the Soviet state lead inevitably to Stalinism? Can we assume that all those questions that I and so many others agonized over have now, in these last months, been fully answered and disposed of? Not likely.

In some countries, we now watch the discredited order and equally discredited myths being giving way to virulent nationalism, ethnic hatreds and enthusiasm for unrestrained *laissez faire*. I fear that the demise of communism is to be accompanied not by the dispelling of the long shadow of history; it is to be accompanied by the erosion of tolerance and of historical memory.

I know that the current historical moment is as splendid as it is unique. But I am also aware of past moments. They include the death of Stalin, Kruschev's speech in 1956, the Hungarian insurrection, the outbreaks of unrest in East Germany and Poland, the Prague Spring, the birth of Solidarity in Poland, the rise of Gorbachev. Each of them was distinct, and each hastened the advent of the present Moment. And I am aware, too, of the deceits bred by faulty memory. Perhaps I owe this awereness to my father, whose bitter brushes with History taught him to suspect facile simplicities, to respect distinctions, and to ponder over unanswered questions. Like his own father, he lived his life in History. So have I. We all do, whether we know it or not.

Noel Annan

In the last few weeks Berlin has haunted my mind. It is the only place where I have taken an active part in an election. That was in the early months of 1946 when elections were to be held in the city and in the Soviet Zone. The Soviet authorities realized that the Communist Party had no hope of winning. So they declared that, to avoid the working classes being split as they had been in 1933, the Social Democrat Party should amalgamate with the Communist Party to form the Socialist Unity Party (SED). In the Soviet Zone the Social Democrats were forced to submit. Anyone who resisted found himself in jail.

But in Berlin things were different. The rank and file of the Social Democrats were against amalgamation, but their leader Otto Grotewohl was a weak, vain man and under pressure from the Russians he announced that his party in Berlin intended to merge with the Communists. He misjudged the temper of the Berlin people. He also misjudged the temper of the Western Allies. My chief, Kit Steel, who later became the British Ambassador to the Federal Republic, asked me to help the Social Democrats, since I was responsible for the development of German political parties. And, with further assistance from my American colleagues, we organized the campaign against amalgamation. In those days no German was allowed to write or say anything that could be construed as criticism of the occupying powers. It therefore was left to me to write articles reminding Berliners of the political record of Ulbricht, the Communist Party leader. Ulbricht in exile had defended the Nazi-Soviet pact, had attacked those who resisted Hitler and had referred to the Social Democrats in approved Party style as social fascists. The delegates of the Social Democrat Party had to meet in the Soviet sector of Berlin to vote. With considerable courage they voted overwhelmingly against the merger.

Thereafter the Communists improved their technique of taking over democracies. Czechoslovakia fell, and in 1948 Stalin decided to eliminate Berlin. Following the Soviet blockade of the city, I returned to Berlin to circumstances which were both dramatic and farcical. Each of the four powers was busy producing cultural manifestations to impress the Berliners. The Russians sent a four-hundred strong Cossack choir to sing in the Alexanderplatz. The British sent madrigal singers from Cambridge and a university drama society to play *Measure for Measure* and *The White Devil* in which I was cast as Cardinal Montecelso. What effect this had on the Berliners I cannot imagine, but despite our acting, their morale rose steadily as the roar of aircraft landing at Tempelhof day and night continued.

The years passed. The Wall was built. When it was breached and the Social Democrats in East Germany finally announced their intention to break away from the Communist Party, the chapter that began for me in the winter of 1945—1946 closed.

My generation grew up in the thirties. We lived under the shadow of a great apocalyptic political movement that divided the culture of Europe as profoundly as the division between Catholics and Protestants in the late-sixteenth and seventeenth century. The debates about dialectical materialism and demand-theory were as bitter as those about the Real Presence and Justification by Faith. It is quite untrue that the most intelligent undergraduates in the thirties were Communists or Marxists, but it is an equal error not to recognize how the Depression, unemployment and the rise of Hitler convinced some of them that the Marxist explanation of these events was right. When Arthur Koestler first read Marx he said the new light seemed 'to pour from all directions across the skull. . . There was now an answer to every question, doubts and conflicts were a matter of the tortured past.'

No one can have a glimmering of the feelings of the left before the war who does not understand its obsession with the Spanish Civil War: it was the only *authentic* war in which the forces for good were ranged against the forces for evil. The war of 1939 was not authentic: Britain was being led by men who had failed to stand up to Fascism. For the left the war became authentic only in 1941. The left rejoiced as the Red Army eliminated the regimes of the kings and regents of Eastern European countries, and spoke with scorn about the Polish officers in London. These intellectuals believed Europe to be on the verge of a people's revolution. Meeting Kingsley Martin when I returned from Berlin at the end of 1946, I found he believed that, but for the Anglo-American armies,

Europe would have been governed by socialist regimes installed by popular acclamation.

In fact this vision of the left bore no relation to the simple desires of human beings in Europe. All they wanted was food and shelter and freedom from the authorities. It is the same today. The people in Eastern Europe have not rebelled in the name of a great cause. They rebelled against the regimentation and dreariness of life. They want the consumer goods of the West and freedom from arbitrary authorities.

There is elation at seeing political prisoners released, secret police headquarters ransacked and, perhaps, Gulags emptied. Communism has lost whatever moral force it had—even the Euro-communism that existed in Italy and in France, in Sartre's day, with its dazzling and bogus pretensions. It has not lost its appeal in the Third World. There will continue to be countries where, exasperated by corrupt dictators and grasping landlords, the peasants and intellectuals become inspired by that bitter hatred of oppression and injustice that moved Marx.

But in Europe everyone seems convinced that the dark ages can never return. I am by nature more sceptical and cynical. The history of reforming czars and progressive ministers in Russia is not encouraging. People still have too great faith in the ability of government to defeat the changes brought about by fortune, and they become disillusioned with its failure to protect them from the chances of fate. Still, this Christmas it is better to hope than to fear.

Günter Kunert

At times of crisis in Germany there is talk of dreams, more so probably than in any other country in the world. Romanticism is a quintessentially German product, a museum piece that has taken on a new relevance with the Wall in Berlin fallen; writers from the East and West, falling suddenly into each other's arms appear to be as Romantic as their eighteenth- and nineteenth-century counterparts. At no time was this more apparent than on 29 November 1989 when a number of authors and intellectuals in East Berlin—among them, Stefan Heym, Volker Braun, Christa Wolf—published an appeal urging people to uphold the 'moral values' of the socialism of the German Democratic Republic and to bring into being a 'new', a 'true', a 'genuine' socialism.

We see today the crowds in Leipzig and East Berlin. They are raging at a system that has cheated them all their lives with its feudal structure of hierarchies. We see people whose most heartfelt desire is for an existence without fear or deprivation—a normal existence. And they are answered by writers and intellectuals who, having never known such deprivation, call for a purified, revitalized socialism.

What is going on in the heads of the authors of this declaration? Who are they? They seem to have set themselves up as the Praeceptor Germaniae, the old German head-teacher, lecturing the children as to what they should and should not do, and the role of lecturer, 'teacher', 'people's educator', is, of course, the favourite pose of the German poet and writer. What is this 'democratic socialism' and how is it supposed to inspire people who have been led around by the nose for forty years? It has little to do with them. Is it nothing more than the untested brainchild of an educated and domineering mentality? The authors of the declaration of 29 November 1989 set themselves up, once again, to dictate how life should be and how we should behave within their hypothetical construct, revealing, thus, their contempt for ordinary people. The ordinary people on the streets of East Germany have not the slightest interest in revitalizing socialism of any sort. They are not asking for a new system; they

161

are asking, understandably, for a better life. And since no one has yet given them a concrete answer, they are now demanding the reunification of Germany as their last hope of rising out of the chaos of a state that has done nothing but exploit them. The intellectuals of course protest that reunification would mean 'selling out' East Germany, reducing it to a colony of the Federal Republic, but their protest hardly matters to the people on the streets. A better life is what matters to them, whatever the flag and whatever the government; no one wants to wait any longer. For forty years they have been fed on empty promises: why should a promise of 'democratic socialism' suddenly satisfy them?

Socialism is finished as an alternative to other systems of society, and it is disappearing from history. It is not yet clear what will take its place. This uncertainty is profoundly disturbing to East German intellectuals, who have always sought to shore themselves up with certainties and absolutes, however fictitious. The German intellectual, one could say in a variation on one of Brecht's Keuner stories, needs a God. He cannot exist without 'isms'. So he shuts his eyes to the facts and clings to a fata morgana made of paper untainted by the filth and blood of reality.

Translated from the German by Harriet Goodman

Tony Benn

Perestroika and glasnost have far-reaching consequences for the thinking of socialists all over the world. What is needed is the emergence of more democratic control, at every level of Soviet society—political and economic, regional and national—if socialism is to remain rooted in the experience of those it is intended to serve. I suspect that some of the most influential pressures for change are coming from the intelligentsia, who were prevented from publishing what they wished; from the media, who suffered under the same restraints; and from the managers, who wished to have greater power. If those are the major forces now at work in the USSR, then working people, as a whole, will have to assert their own determination not to fall under the control of a new group of governors, in the name of reform.

Having said that, it is also important to recognize the immense achievements of the Soviet government since 1917. It was the first workers' state in the world. It pioneered huge advances in education and health, in housing and social welfare. The Soviet Union assisted liberation movements in every continent, and the immense sacrifices made by its own people during the Second World War made possible the defeat of Fascism.

In recent years the Gorbachev initiatives in the field of disarmament have put the NATO strategists on the defensive, and given the peace movement in the West the opening it has needed to press for more positive responses and a reduction of the arms burden. People have always tended to be sceptical about disarmament plans, suspecting that they were merely propaganda moves to embarrass another country. But when Gorbachev made it clear that he wanted disarmament to ease the burden of his arms budget and to improve the living standards of the Soviet people, the reaction in Britain was 'We want to do the same.' In Britain today Gorbachev is far more popular than Reagan or Bush.

I can visualize the development of a form of democracy, inside the USSR, which permits a popular choice of leaders, each of whom is committed to upholding socialism, in much the same way as in the West the political parties vying for power are, in effect, competing for the privilege of running capitalism.

Czesław Miłosz

What will happen next? Does the victory of the multi-party system in the countries of Central and Eastern Europe mean the end of their estrangement from the West? Will they, by introducing the classical division of powers—a legislature, executive and judiciary—recognize the supremacy of all Western values? Will the years of suffering under totalitarian rule be obliterated, erased and the people start from scratch? Should the thinkers, poets and artists join their Western colleagues in the somewhat marginal role assigned to them in societies busy with selling and buying?

These questions are important, for they have to do with the deeper meaning of the twentieth century. For many decades the two blocs followed different cultural paths: the Western open, the Eastern clandestine. Fulfilling Friedrich Nietzsche's prophecy about 'European nihilism' Western thought and art did not offer us, in the East, much nourishment. Most Western writers seemed frivolous and irresponsible; measured by artistic exigencies, they appeared as indifferent to a hierarchy of quality and of taste. Most Western film and television makers shocked us by their hare-brainedness and lack of concern for the needs of human imagination, which gets dulled by being constantly exposed to scenes of violence and perversion. We did not respect the leading English, French and American intellectuals who praised the ugly totalitarian reality from a distance. We shrugged when their names, be it Bernard Shaw or Jean-Paul Sartre, were mentioned. We in the East knew the words Auschwitz and Bergen-Belsen, but the West did not learn Kolyma, Vorkuta, Katyn.

The failure of Marx's vision has created the need for another vision, not for a rejection of all visions. I do not speak of 'socialism with a human face', for that belongs to the past. I speak instead about a concern with society, civilization and humanity in a period when the nineteenth-century idea of progress has died out and a related idea, communist revolution, has disintegrated. What remains today is the idea of responsibility, which works against the loneliness and indifference of an individual living in the belly of a whale. Together with historical memory, the belief in personal responsiblity has contributed to the Solidarity movement in Poland, the national fronts in the Baltic States, the Civic Forum in Czechoslovakia. I hope that the turmoil in these countries has not been a temporary phase, a passage to an ordinary society of earners and consumers, but rather the birth of a new form of human interaction, of a non-utopian style and vision.

Ivan Klíma

The first pictures of the Prague demonstration of 17 November were of young girls placing flowers on shields held by riot police. Later the police got rough, but their furious brutality failed to provoke a single violent response. Not one car was damaged, not one window smashed during daily demonstrations by hundreds of thousands of people. Posters stuck up on the walls of houses, in metro stations, on shop windows and in trams by the striking students called for peaceful protest. Flowers became the symbol of Civic Forum.

It is only recently that we have seen the fragility of totalitarian power. Is it really possible that a few days of protest—unique in the history of revolutions for their peacefulness—could topple a regime which had harassed our citizens for four decades?

The rest of the world had all but forgotten the 1968 invasion of Czechoslovakia by the armies of five countries. Even now, our nation has barely recovered from that invasion; what did not recover was the leading force in the country, the Communist Party. By subsequently making approval of the invasion and the occupation a condition of membership, the Party deprived itself of almost all patriotic and worthy members, becoming for the rest of the nation a symbol of moral decay and betrayal. The government, then stripped of its authority and its intelligence, went on to devastate the country culturally, morally and materially. An economically mature country fell back among the developing countries, while achieving a notable success in atmospheric pollution, incidence of malignant tumours and short life expectancy.

Unrestrained power breeds arrogance. And arrogance threatens not only the subject but also the ruler. In Czechoslovakia the ruling party, deprived of an élite and of any outstanding personalities, combined arrogance with provocative stupidity. It persisted obstinately in defending the occupation of Czechoslovakia, indeed as an act of deliverance at a time when even the invaders themselves were re-examining their past. The government actually went so far as to suggest that the apologies offered by the Polish and Hungarian governments for their role in the invasion constituted interference in the internal affairs of the country. How could the nation consider such a government as its own? The months leading up to the events of November, however static they may have seemed compared with the agitation in the neighbouring countries, were in fact a period of waiting for circumstances for change. The regime, unable to discern its utter isolation, in relation to both its own nation and the community of nations, reacted in its usual manner to a peaceful demonstration to commemorate the death of a student murdered by the Nazis fifty years ago. It could not have picked a worse moment—the patience of the silent nation had snapped; the circumstances had finally changed.

We, who had consistently tried to show the bankruptcy of the regime, were surprised at how quickly it collapsed under the blows of that one weapon, truth, voiced by demonstrators—students and actors who immediately went to the country to win over people— and then spread by a media no longer willing to serve a mendacious and brutal regime. As such non-violence was the only weapon we needed to use against violent power. Will those who were robbed, harassed and humiliated continue to be so magnanimous? As long as they can be they have in their power to realize the idea of a democratic Europe, a Europe for the next millennium, a Europe of nations living in mutual domestic peace.

Translated from the Czech by Daphne Dorrell

Stephen Spender

Perhaps because I am eighty what is happening today in the Soviet Union, East Germany, Czechoslovakia, Hungary and Bulgaria has the effect of making me feel that I am witnessing apocalyptic events out of the Book of Revelations. I do not apologize for beginning on this personal note. For the collapse of the totalitarian regimes in the Soviet Union and Eastern Europe is something that I had given up hope of witnessing in my lifetime. I was sure that it would happen eventually but that it would be perpetually postponed to the next century, after the millennium. I now have the almost Biblical sense of being privileged to witness a miracle.

Perhaps some young people have the same kind of feeling. A historic event may seem to contemporaries part of a larger impersonal history being unfolded before their eyes, and yet at the same time strike each separately as being his or her intensely felt personal experience. The assassination of President Kennedy had this effect on thousands of people who, notoriously almost, remember what they were doing at the moment when they heard the news of Kennedy's death.

Judging from the newspapers, many people in the West—especially conservative politicians—take what they call 'the end of communism' to signify the defeat of the evil Communist Satan and the triumph of the Capitalist God in a Manichean struggle between the forces of Good (Capitalism) and of Evil (Communism). This seems to me a dangerously false reading of recent events. What has triumphed is Democracy, the will of the people, and in a very unideological, politically scarcely realized, form. And this is not because socialism ('socialism with a human face') has failed but because Marxist ideology, tied to the concept of 'the dictatorship of the proletariat', has broken down.

The evil of communism is that Marxist leaders, beginning with Lenin, believed that any means justified the end of overcoming capitalism. Communist leaders everywhere became corrupt as a consequence of their having absolute power. But today, when the corruption of the older generation of communist leaders in East Germany is exposed, it is perhaps salutary to remember that in their youth many of these leaders were heroic idealists (though preaching 'historical materialism'). They were opponents of Hitler, and several were killed or imprisoned, ending their lives in concentration camps. Ernst Thaelmann, the German communist leader, murdered by the Nazis in Buchenwald concentration camp in August 1944, would almost certainly be in the same position as his follower Erich Honecker, if he were alive today.

Perhaps it is too simple to read these events in terms of the political divisions which have dominated nations in the twentieth century. Of course resurgent nationalism and shortage of consumer goods help produce a revolutionary situation, but there is a historically unprecedented negative factor which seems to me tremendously important, especially among students and intellectuals. This might be called 'the boredom factor'. Life under a dictatorship of old-style ideologists, whether in Russia, Eastern Europe or China, is extremely boring. Moreover, owing to modern systems of communication people living under dictatorships are made aware of the boredom of the system: the flow of information from the outside is unstoppable. The Berlin Wall may have prevented East Berliners reaching the West, but it was leaped over and penetrated at a million points by TV and radio bringing East Berliners news and images of the lifestyle, vitality and competitiveness of the West.

Commentators have had difficulty defining, in political terms of left or right, the changes taking place in the communist world today. Apart from nationalism and very pressing economic problems the movement is perhaps more a cultural than a clearly definable political revolution. It is led by intellectuals and students who know what they want—freedom of self-expression and removal of the dead weight of censorship and Party dogma—better than they know the politics which they wish to see replace Communism.

The crowds of rejoicing young people who have got rid of their communist party leaders have streamed across the TV screens of Western Europe. Mass demonstrations proved their point when they were seen by a world in moving photographs. Violence had become superfluous and unnecessary. No one needed to be killed, and no Bastilles stormed. This theatre is the living truth of the liberation movements. It is significant that Vaclav Havel is a playwright. His Civic Forum has the look of characters in search of a party and a policy. What we see may show that we have moved beyond the nineteenth- and twentieth-century cycle of revolutions—murder followed by counter-revolutions, also murderous—to a period when great political-cultural changes are acts of recognition of changed states of consciousness among people, made apparent as *faits accomplis* by the mass media.

But that is to look far beyond the present, into the twenty-first century. Many things may go wrong. Gorbachev may fail and be succeeded by the military. Problems caused by mass starvation may supersede all others and may produce widespread death and violence. Nevertheless the recent events have shown that dictatorial regimes are incapable of replacing an old leadership with youthful leaders without the regimes and their ideology crumbling. There were signs of this in 1968 when the movement forward in communist societies was reversed in Czechoslovakia by Soviet troops. It is difficult to believe that a reversal, if it happens, will be as effective—not even in China. If the present revolution is stopped in any one place, to be superseded by dictatorship, the media will assure that the consciousness of a democratic world, flooding in, will sooner or later break down the prison walls of the dictatorship.

Mercea Dinescu

Not long ago, in the icy Siberian plains, a few hard-frozen mammoths were discovered. The discoverers were astonished to find camomile flowers inside their bellies. I recalled the incident when I came upon an article in the Western press entitled 'Last Stalinist mammoth left in Romania.' I greatly fear that, when the social climate in Romania does change, we will not find any camomile flowers inside the belly of our Stalinist beast, but several dead bodies. People from the Jiu valley, from Barsov, Timişoara, Cluj, Iaşi, Tirgu Mures, and Bucharest have been and are still being swallowed alive. They are people about whom little, or even nothing at all, is known, who were courageous enough to vent their exasperation, even if only within their communities.

Who will intervene in Romania? God does not get involved in politics. I hope I will be forgiven for saying that our daily prayer does not seem to have been heard. Our priests have been forced into becoming trade unionists in cassocks. The 'accidental' deaths of a few troublesome priests, as well as the 'lay' pressure applied by the civilian representatives of the Secu Monastery to the more talkative members of the clergy, have introduced permanent terror into the holy orders. There are no Polish-style Catholic shipyards or factories in our country. There is no militant church, no icon to work miracles like the one in Czestochowa. Our icons are of the president; our factories are run by soldiers; and our churches have, in the winter, the highest number of funerals in the world.

Where can we go now that the Berlin Wall is being preserved, brick by brick, and transpored to the Romanian border? Who will come to our defence? The lawyers, the men who studied the force and superiority of the 'Romanian Left' over the 'Roman Right' at the Law Faculty, are reduced to a state of powerlessness and obedience. They are so afraid of losing their jobs that they have come to consider the Romanian constitution as a mere propaganda instrument, a tool of the devil which cannot, therefore, really help you when it comes down to it. In a moment of desperation and rebellion, a former schoolfriend pasted up a few anti-president notices at Bucharest's main railway station, and was condemned to five years' imprisonment. The worse attack against him was made, during the closed trial, by his defence lawyer.

Can we appeal to the popular militia? The strong, ruddy-cheeked lads stand in their fine uniforms at every ten metres on the streets of Bucharest. As they stare at the population they seem to be looking at a flock of helpless sheep. During their brief training, they have learned that anyone moving after ten at night, when the street lights go off, and when the cinemas, the restaurants and the theatres close—the hour, that is, when Romanian towns die—must be a criminal, or at the very least an evil pyromaniac, about to set fire to Lenin's statue, which was in fact burned last year.

Can we look to the members of the press for support—those apostles of the personality cult? For twenty years our newspapers have been re-using the same poorly reprinted photographs and the same meaningless sentences. The only space which provides any real information is the obituaries. In any case, it seems that the good journalists died with everyone else in the Second World War.

What about glasnost? Will anything come of Soviet openness? I do not know why it should be, but the window through which the Moscow press views Romania is quite hazy. Like an eclipse you cannot actually see anything through it. I have the impression that it is through General Jaruzelski's black glasses that Gorbachev is looking at Romania.

What of the dissidents? You do hear the odd squeak from them now and then, but so seldom that it makes you wonder if Romanians—there would appear to be only one dissident for every two million inhabitants here—are by nature more silent than the Germans, the Hungarians or the Poles. I have been preoccupied recently by another thought, though: that, paradoxically, the regime may be keeping our extremely small number of dissidents alive for propaganda purposes. Now that the Western press and human rights organizations have realized that the dissidents exist, it is too late to get rid of them. But this isn't the case. In actual fact there are twenty million protesters in Romania, unpublicized dissidents who live their lives gagged. I never heard about any anti-fascist demonstrations on the streets of Berlin in the 1940s. In the streets there was order and discipline; it was only in their homes that people whispered.

In our country political trials are not possible for the simple reason that it is written clearly in the constitution that a citizen has the right to freedom of opinions. Furthermore, a Party statute specifies that any member of the Party may criticize anyone else—even the General Secretary. A repressive organization operates undercover. Once marked as protester, you must learn to be careful—not to walk alone in town, for instance, or to let your children play outside. You must take care to disinfect your door handle thoroughly; it may be poisoned.

The situation in our country cannot be compared with anywhere in the world. When I heard that Václav Havel had a television and word processor in his Prague prison, I thought it was a joke. In Romania a writer is not allowed to have a typewriter in his own home without permission from the police. A Romanian dissident, a poet, was given the choice between three months in prison, spent in the company of hardened criminals waiting for some young lads to come along, or emigration. The writer chose exile.

How were most writers corrupted? In the 1950s a privileged élite emerged. With one poem published on the front page of the Party newspaper, you could buy an English-made overcoat and eat in the best restaurant in Bucharest for a whole month. What glorious times! 'Pelisor', once the luxurious residence of King Carol, became known as the 'House of Creators' for all those rolling off the conveyer belt of the new writing factories. History was standing on its head: the proletarian-culture poets were sprawling on what was once Queen Maria's bed, composing illiterate but enthusiastic 'revolutionary' poems. With a 'heigh-ho' and a 'praise Stalin' vineyards were sold off and some people got very rich. Millionaires appeared from the ranks of the Party writers. Ever since then it has been this kind of literary activist, buckled under the weight of so many privileges, who has been chosen to lead the artists and be their spokesman.

In the 1960s, the censors relaxed for a short time. In the years that followed, however, at a time when writers were not showing much enthusiasm for the new cultural revolution, imported from China, the confiscations and repressions began. Pelisor was once more turned into the new princes' summer residence; poems regained their symbolic value. Authors' photographs were removed from the covers of their books for fear of encouraging—God forbid—a personality cult. At the same time it was argued that the Writers' Union should be disbanded as it was a relic from the old system, an organization based on the Soviet model. Everything else, our transport system, our food packaging, was built on Japanese, American or French models.

Writers briefly manifested a sign of life in 1981, when, at a national conference, many of their voices sounded a little out of key from the tune the central authorities were singing. But their Union has long been undermined by the ineffective, passive resistance of some of its most prominent members, and by the vacuum left by the mass emigration of disillusioned writers. It has metamorphosed into a sort of co-operative making completely alien products.

Although the spectre of poverty hovers over the majority of Romanian writers today—even while the number of lucrative homages to the state have been increasing every month—a general strike is what is called for. A general strike of all writers would be the easiest solution for saving the face of Romanian culture. If they were to all speak with one voice, the mammoths of today would feed on camomile and perish.

Translated from the Romanian by Fiona Tupper-Carey

YURI RIBCHINSKY
WEDDING DAY

First published in *Die Zeitgenössische Photographie in der Sowjetunion*. Edition Stemmle, Schaffhausen.

MIKHAIL
STEBLIN-KAMENSKY
THE SIEGE OF
LENINGRAD

Alexander Ivanovich woke at six, the hour when radio broadcasting would normally have begun, but the radio had been silent for a month now. He lay still for a long while, covered in blankets and furs. The room was dark and very cold. He thought that this was probably how things had been a thousand years ago, the period he specialized in as a philologist; that this was how people lived in medieval towns, without running water, sewers, electricity, newspapers or radio. Life in the age of devastating epidemics, famines, enemy invasions and endless sieges had been exactly as it was in Leningrad today. Alexander Ivanovich had often tried to picture the medieval town in a time of plague, siege or invasion. He had imagined streets where skulking dogs gnawed at human corpses, while untended fires smoked around them. Now these dreams had become a reality more prosaic than anything he had been able to conceive. Alexander Ivanovich tried to convince himself that he had been presented with a singular opportunity to observe life at its most strange and remote, but the thought gave him no satisfaction. He took some matches from under the pillow, lit the lamp, threw on his coat, pulled on his boots and began to kindle a fire in the small iron stove with wood from a bookcase sawn up the night before.

His sister woke; they had been living together in one room since her husband had left for the Front. Alexander Ivanovich placed a pot of water—the last of it—on the stove. He opened a drawer in the table and took out a morsel of bread. It was carefully wrapped in white paper. Alexander Ivanovich would have recognized this morsel in a thousand. For a rouble and ten kopecks a loaf, the bread was spongy but not crumbly; it sliced easily and stuck to the fingers. Alexander Ivanovich cut off the crust, crumbled a pulp into the pot with his fingers and liberally added salt. Then he sat down in front of the stove, opened its door and

---

The Siege of Leningrad began in November 1941, after 500,000 German troops had entered the Soviet Union. The siege ended two-and-a-half years later, on 27 January 1944, when Russians broke out of the city and reached the Gulf of Finland, 750,000 people died.

began reading a Greek grammar by the light of the flame.

'The aorist,' he read, 'often denotes an action, of some duration, but referred to in its completion, without special expression of duration, as for example in Herodotus: "The town of Azot resisted [fact referred to in its completion] longer than all the other towns." The aorist may also denote a general fact, if the given action is not referred to in its development, but only as a fact, capable of being repeated an infinite number of times, as for example in Theognis': "The slow but cunning man will overtake the swift man."'

None of this was of any use, but he absorbed it easily.

He put a broken chair-leg and a piece of plywood into the stove, the flame blazed up and he returned to his book. Then he stirred the watery broth and crushed the tiny pieces of bread floating in the water. He added more firewood, so that the flame was kept strong and the hob was hottest directly beneath the pot. It would have been difficult for him to part with his burning stove for even a short time. All the same, it was time to go for water.

To fetch water he had to go three houses down, where a stream of water was still running from an iced-up tap. He took a pail in one hand and, in the other, a saucepan with a piece of string fastened on as a handle. At the entrance to the cellar, in a snow-covered courtyard flooded with sewage, there was a queue of people who stood rigid in the cold: sexless and ageless, muffled up in anything they could lay hands on, clutching pails, saucepans, bowls and pitchers. It was going to be a long wait. To make the time pass, Alexander Ivanovich counted to himself: one, two, three, four, five, six, seven, eight, and, losing count, he started again: one, two, three, four, five, six . . . He was sure it would be warmer in the cellar. But when he reached the wet cement floor, amid the clanking of pails and the abuse shouted at people who had slipped and spilled their water or who had lost their place in the queue, it was no better. His boots were soaking and icy, and his hands seemed to have frozen on to the iron handle of the saucepan; it was no longer possible to think of anything but food. He filled the pail and pulled it out of the washing-trough with difficulty, spilling some of it as he did so. He climbed the icy steps slowly, afraid of spilling more water. His felt boots were large and clumsy and seemed to step independently of his will. They reminded him of the boots worn by figures depicted on the lid of a thousand-year-old reliquary, familiar to him from illustrations in books.

'I was beginning to think something had happened to you,' his sister said when he returned. After letting him in, she went out on to the landing; she was waiting for a letter from her husband at the Front, and she shook the letter-box and peered into it through the slot, but it was empty. They went into their room. While Alexander had been away she had thrown herself into the housework and her face, although emaciated and wrinkled was flushed and looked youthful. She told him what she had managed to do: she had taken out the slop pails and hacked the frozen sewage out of them, tidied the room, hung a carpet over the bottom half of the window to block out the draught, carried a little crockery shelf in from the kitchen and put it down by the stove, washed the linen, ground up some salt and even, as she announced with particular triumph, found a little packet of chicory in the cupboard which turned out to be extremely tasty.

She poured the soup into two bowls and put the fuller one in front of Alexander Ivanovich.

'I ate a few spoonfuls while I was stirring it. I was so hungry I could hardly stop myself eating the lot,' she said.

The soup was pale brown, glutinous, bubbly and left a slime on the spoon. It was hot and salty and had a slightly sour taste. Alexander Ivanovich ate with a dessert-spoon instead of a table-spoon so that the process of eating might last longer. When he had finished he licked the plate and spoon, and picked the crumbs off the table and ate them too. There was nothing left. All that remained was the wait for the evening bowl of soup, the evening morsel of bread.

'You should go to the clinic, to renew your medical card,' said his sister, 'and I'll help Dima bury his mother. She must still be lying in the same room as him.'

'You shouldn't bother.'

'I want to help him. Dima can hardly stand on his feet and has probably survived so far thanks to her. When I met her the last time, I thought she'd gone mad. She said she had a dead rat in her bag "for Dimka". She found it somewhere near the front gates. I don't know whether they ate that rat. They'd already eaten their cat.'

'Does it really matter where, or even whether, she's buried?' said Alexander Ivanovich.

'It doesn't matter to you, but it matters to him.'

'It doesn't matter to him. He doesn't feel anything except hunger. You should save your strength and not waste it on nothing.'

In the entrance hall of the clinic a man with a padded hat and blue lips was sitting on the floor by a bench. A woman was pushing breadcrumbs into his mouth. As Alexander Ivanovich walked past them, they collapsed on to the floor. A nurse drove them out of the hall. 'They come here to die,' she said indignantly, 'and then you're landed with them. Every day there are dead people lying here on the bench.'

Again the wait among sexless, ageless beings, muffled up in dirty rags, faces sooty from their stoves. Again he could only number the seconds, try not to think of food.

A creature muffled up in a hood, with feverish, glittering eyes, was spreading delirious rumours: They've run the blockade, they've taken Pskov, they've taken Luga, the war will soon be over, there'll be an increase of bread from the first of the month, they'll be giving everyone sanatorium rations, a hundred carriages have arrived bringing provisions for the people of Leningrad. As the creature spoke, a louse climbed along its hood. Alexander Ivanovich noticed it and moved away.

He returned home. Every time he passed a sled coming in the opposite direction, carrying something wrapped up or wound up like a mummy, Alexander Ivanovich would glance at it with curiosity; it always turned out to be what he thought it was. He counted fourteen sleds before he reached home. One corpse was being carried on a child's pram, which bumped and jolted along the ruts in the road. And the living people coming towards him walked like corpses, if corpses could walk; they clutched walking-sticks in outstretched hands; their bodies were bent as though their centre of gravity had moved somewhere higher than usual; their faces had no expression.

It was dark by the time he arrived home. In a neighbouring part of the city a five-storey building was on fire. Who knows how the fire had started. There hadn't been any incendiary bombs for a while now.

He recalled one of the medieval chronicles in which, alongside a record of the kings and bishops, the soldiers killed in battle and the laconic accounts of invasion, famine and epidemic, the writer had noted that in that year a fire-breathing dragon had flown over the land. The event had apparently been no more out of the ordinary than the burning down of a monastery, the murder of one of the king's retinue or the arrival of an embassy from a far-off kingdom.

Alexander Ivanovich listened to the irregular shell bursts. About a minute went by between each explosion, although from time to time two shells would suddenly explode in quick succession. The windows rattled slightly, but he did not seem to be in any danger; a different area was being shelled, perhaps the Vyborg side or some part of the city further off. Alexander Ivanovich got up, lit the stove, put the soup on to boil and sat down in front of the open stove door with his Greek grammar. 'In Greek,' he read, 'the stem of the present tense denotes an action referred to in its development, in its duration; but the stem of the aorist signifies a single action. Let us take the following phrase from Xenophon: "They fought [process referred to in its development, in its duration] until the Athenians set sail," which draws attention only to the very fact of their setting sail and therefore uses the aorist.' All the wood in the stove had burned. Alexander Ivanovich stood up and tasted the soup with a spoon. He ate a whole spoonful and then another. Then he took the morsel of bread that had been saved for the evening meal and cut a thin slice. 'I'm a weak man,' he thought, 'despite the fact that I understand the Greek aorist.'

His sister didn't arrive home until much later. The embers in the stove had long burned out. A strong draught was blowing through the window and through the door with the carpet hanging over it. Alexander Ivanovich lay in the darkness and counted the seconds. There was a knock at the door.

'Did you bury her?'

'Yes. It was dreadful coming back. I took Dima home—he

could hardly walk. The streets are deserted.'

'Why did you go? It's not like you. What would it have mattered if the militia had come and taken her? You have to save your strength.'

This made her angry and she told him to stop. But then after a silence she said: 'The things I've seen! You can't imagine what I've seen.'

'Eat!'

She pulled a plate towards her and told her story: 'She was lying on a bed in the corner, under a blanket. I didn't recognize their rooms at all. There were pots and bottles and bits and pieces all over the place, pulled out of cupboards which had been broken up for firewood. Everything was black with soot from the stove. On the bed there was a kind of den made of coats and furs. And the stench from the slop pail—he's got diarrhoea. I took the slop pail out for him and brought in water. He wrapped Maria Nikolaevna up and dragged her down on a sled and took her to the park. Dima insisted that we did not go to the cemetery. He'd seen a notice saying there would be a "collection of corpses" by the militia in the park. When we got there they were already heaping them on to a lorry. It was piled high. The women loading it were in a hurry and didn't want to take any more. One said she was sick of the dead. When the lorry moved off, a corpse fell out on to the snow and rolled out of its blanket—well, something filthy anyway, not really a blanket or a curtain. And two corpses were just left there on the ground. Then Dima said maybe he did want to take her to the cemetery after all. He could barely stand on his feet; I had to support him. He kept saying we weren't going to survive anyway. I assured him it wouldn't be long now. And you know, I so wanted to convince him that we would survive that I believed it myself and he seemed to believe it too. So many corpses were being taken there. Very few of them were in coffins, most were just wrapped up. As we were crossing the river we passed the corpse of a woman lying unwrapped with the thigh hacked out. Cut out for meat. Along the embankment I counted nineteen discarded corpses. My hands were frozen. We dragged ourselves to the cemetery; by now it was totally dark. There was some kind of hut in the graveyard. It was dark inside and the stove was lit and there was a delicious smell of broth.

The women who dig graves for bread were sitting there. I could hardly see them—the only light in the hut came from the stove—one of them was eating a piece of bread. Can you imagine? Not like we eat—a great hunk of bread! She wasn't even bothering to pick up the crumbs. And they didn't give a damn; they were having a laugh. And everywhere there's darkness, frost and corpses, corpses, dragged along, thrown by the roadside . . . ' She fell silent.

That's how it was, thought Alexander Ivanovich, in medieval towns in times of hunger or plague; mass graves grew up around the churches; there were still reminders of them in Novgorod. Only in those days it had seemed normal and inevitable, and there was no comparison to be made with any other possible reality. Just as it hadn't seemed out of the ordinary when a fire-breathing dragon had flown over the town. Of course, what was happening now was incomparably more terrible.

Alexander Ivanovich sat at the table while his sister cleared it and put away the plates. Outside on the street stood the houses of the dead, with no light in their windows; corpses in rags lay in gateways, on the snow and in the sewage-flooded public squares among hoar-frosted trees; there wasn't a living soul in sight.

Alexander Ivanovich wasn't thinking about any of that. He was devising a justification for having cut a thin slice off the morsel of bread saved for the morning, from the unevenly cut side where the edge of the crust was sticking out. But he was unable to devise a justification so he gave up and began to get ready for bed. He took off his felt boots and laid them on the cooling stove to dry. The boots seemed to stand there like a man whose head and body had been destroyed or disappeared, leaving nothing but his feet, drawing the vital warmth from the cooling iron of the stove.

Translated from the Russian by Rachel Polonsky

Note: 'The Dragon' was written in 1943, but first published, in *Neva*, No. 1, in 1989.

VLADIMIR FILONOV
DYING VILLAGE

First published in *Die Zeitgenössische Photographie in der Sowjetunion*, Edition Stemmle, Schaffhausen.

JOSEPH BRODSKY
DEMOCRACY

The offices of the leader of a small socialist state.

Interior: the apotheosis of dullness, enlivened only by a full-sized stuffed bear, in whose direction the actors nod or glance whenever the pronoun 'they' is used.

On the walls: portraits of the founding fathers. High windows, Regency-styled, curtained in white. The spires of Lutheran churches can be discerned through the curtains.

A long conference table, in the centre of which portions of watermelon on a dish glow ruby-red.

The leader's desk: a jumble of telephones.

Noon.

Three middle-aged men and one woman—age indeterminate— are tucking into a meal. They include: Basil Modestovich, Head of State; Petrovich, Minister of the Interior; Gustav Adolfovich, Finance Minister; Cecilia, Minister of Culture; Matilda, Secretary. The speakers are not indicated. The actors and director should decide for themselves who says what, according to the logic of the proceedings.

Not bad, this grouse, eh?

Just right.

It's the gravy, though, that does it.

The gravy's super. What's this in it? Caviar?

Uh-huh. Look's like. Astrakhan, is it?

Guryev.

Guryev, Guryev . . . Where's that over there? Europe, or Asia?

The Urals. They brew good beer there. Makes the legs wobbly, especially in summer.

The grouse is from the Salsky steppes as well, by the way.

The word is Eurasia.

Asiopa, more like, considering the ratio.

N-yes. Siberian furs.

Matches are Swedish.

French perfume.

Dutch cheese.

Turkish tobacco.

No, Bulgarian.

Eh, same difference.

German shepherds.

Roman law.

Everything's foreign.

N-yes. The guards are from Vologda, though.

Handcuffs are American, incidentally. From Pittsburgh, Pennsylvania.

Never!

Honestly.

You can believe him, Cecilia. He's the minister of justice, after all.

Want me to show you? I always carry a set with me in the briefcase. There, feast your eyes on that.

Ooh! No!

Don't be afraid. They're American.

Let's have a look, Petrovich.

Here, it says, 'Made in USA.'

So they've got them too.

What did you think? Capitalism is the word. We don't make this kind of stuff here. Got to lay out foreign currency. Well, no begrudging a good cause.

No begrudging what?

Currency, of course. Expensive, though. Twenty dollars apiece. That's retail, but even in bulk discount, it's dear.

Discount?

Mm-hmm, twenty per cent. 'Most favoured nation.'

Favoured nation?

You can believe him, Cecilia. Finance minister, after all.

Perfume would be a better buy, then. It's French, no less.

They make do with Polish.

Not to mention the name's being so pretty: Pear Hops. That's perhaps in our language.

Otherwise it's Coty.

Coty's pretty as well.

Besides, the French don't give you a discount, Cecilia. And you can never lay in enough perfume for everybody, can you? Even Polish. Perfume goes like nothing else, you know. A vial a week. The currency reserves just couldn't cope. As an investment handcuffs are more sound. From the fiscal point of view, I mean.

Yes, our people are a tame lot. Rope does the job.

Basil Modestovich, could I have a bit of watermelon?

Go ahead. That watermelon's from Astrakhan as well, incidentally.

I don't know about tame. Didn't you see that demonstration yesterday?

The independence one?

For ecology.

Well, it's the same thing.

You can't say that. Ecology is for protecting the environment.

Independence is protection as well, from the same environment, by the way.

Now, you're going a bit too far, Petrovich.

That wasn't me, Boris Modestovich. That was the demonstrators.

Demonstrators, my foot. Just a mob.

Eh, don't say that. It's the people, you know, the masses.

Well, the masses always take the shape of a mob. Or a queue.

That's right: squares or streets. Never anything else.

Let me take that down.

Ah, why bother? It's being done anyway. (*Nods towards the bear.*)

But in that case why do they always rush to the palace? Seen too many movies?

Because there's a square in front of the palace, that's why. And it's a street that leads to the square. As long as they're in the street, they're a queue. When they hit the square, they're a mob. You get both.

Right, no agony of choosing.

There is a third possibility, of course: storming the palace, as in the movies.

Who on earth's going to let them in? It's not 1917. Besides, there are guards behind every tree, not to mention the columns.

As well as inside them.

Right. They are not so much Doric as Trojan.

Ramses. Since they have been renovated. The columns now house surface-to-air missiles.

Nobody'll let them near the portico!

And even if they do get in, there's not enough room for them. Besides the movie was in black and white, you should know that, Cecilia.

Oh, yes, you're right Basil Modestovich, but, you see, in the evenings, the colours blur. Not to mention night. Art always has a greater impact in the evening. They always do Swan Lake after hours, for example. Plays as well. And as for movies, people always watch those in the dark.

You may be right, Cecilia, but people don't demonstrate after dark. They demonstrate in the daytime.

Yes, of course, so Western reporters can take pictures. Videos especially.

Becher cabled the other day from Japan. They've invented a new super-sensitive film. In no time, that press gent is going to feel like Eisenstein.

Oh, come off it. How is Becher doing over there, by the way? Homesick?

He is, Basil Modestovich. Says they make him eat raw fish. That's the Japs for you. Can I have a piece of watermelon?

Go ahead, Petrovich.

Pity they don't grow here.

Can't have everything. We have to pay the price for our geographical advantage. It is Europe, after all.

That's what Beria figured, too. When I was assigned here, I objected. He just said, What's the matter, Petrovich. It is Europe, after all.

Yes, six hours by train and you're in Czechoslovakia. Or in Hungary.

A knock on the door; the secretary enters.

Well, what is it, Matilda?

Basil Modestovich, you're wanted on the phone.

How many times do I have to tell you, Matilda? Not during lunch.

Yes, but it's them on the line.

Who?

I don't know, Basil Modestovich. Somebody with an accent.

Oh, all right. Send it through, Matilda. [*Exit Matilda.*] Gustav Adolfovich, have you finished? You answer it, eh? Talk with an accent.

What sort of accent, Basil Modestovich?

Any sort. Estland.

[*Gustav Adolfovich goes over to the desk and looks irresolutely at the telephones.*] Which one? The red one, I suppose.

What else?

[*Gustav Adolfovich lifts the receiver.*] Ja-a! Thees ees Gustaf Atolfovich . . . Pliss? Nein, ees Finance Minister. Nein, he ist eating. Excuse pliss? What deed you say? Ach, ein moment . . . [*Puts down the receiver and crosses to the table.*] Basil Modestovich, he's shouting. He called me—Cecilia, cover your ears—a cunt buster. It's a Georgian accent, though . . .

[*Basil Modestovich leaps to his feet.*] Comrade Generalissimo! . . . Ugh. No, it can't be. [*Wipes his sweating forehead.*] Petrovich, you go if you've finished, eh? They think they can ring up any time they like. Sheer bad manners, not to mention sovereignty.

[*Petrovich goes over to the desk, picks up the phone.*] 'Allo, Jan Peters speaking. Ivan Petrovich to you. Minister of Justice. Mm-hmm. Yes, of the Interior, for you. What? Becher is Foreign Affairs, right, and he's in Japan. Eh? . . . Just keep your hair on, you've been told he's having his lunch . . . Stop shouting. Cool it, won't you? Yes, yes, with him, me and the Minister of Culture. Mm-hmm, from Tambov. What was that? Yes, best legs in Eastern Europe. [*Looks in Cecilia's direction and winks.*] What? Ha, ha, ha! Never . . . Ha, ha, ha, ha . . . No, never together after dark. Ha, ha, ha . . . A real *mensch*! Yes, all right then—urgent. Urgent, urgent. Where's Himself, then? Ah, press conference. Why didn't you say so straight away? Ah yes, I see. OK, I'll try for you. [*Petrovich lays down the phone and returns to the table.*] That was Wogachvili, Basil Modestovich, their foreign minister. He's asking for you. Actually, according to protocol, he hasn't the authority to do that. Only Himself can call you to the phone. A minister can only ring a minister, and then only his counterpart. It looks as if something's up over there. And Becher's in Japan. Do you want to speak to him?

Yesus Maria! They won't let a man eat in peace! All right, tell him I'm coming in a minute. Just as soon as I cut myself a bit of watermelon.

[*Petrovich goes over to the phone and picks up the receiver.*] 'Allo? He's on his way, it's against protocol, though. Yes, even us. I recall you were interior minister at one time, though, in Tiflis there, no? Mm-hmm, see, I remember. It was under you, then, that they used to sodomize anyone who wouldn't sing. Sure, sure. They're a proud lot in the Caucasus. No, I'm from Ryazan. What? No, I was at the Tank Academy in Kharkov. No, I married a local girl. You what? Homesick, yes, but there's no getting away from here, not even a holiday. What? Their language you mean? Not bad, I can chatter a bit. Mm-hmm, he's coming, he's coming. And where's Himself? Press conference. Ah well, I see. No, here he is. Mm-hmm, well, so long! Good man! Here he is.

[*Petrovich gives the receiver to Basil Modestovich and returns to the table; Basil Modestovich wipes his lips with a napkin.*] Yes, hello. Yes, it's me. Good day to you. Yes, yes, thank you. No, no, not at all. We'd already finished. Good heavens, no! Yes, so what is it then? [*Pause.*] Mein Gott! When? [*Pause.*] Does the ambassador know? No, not ours, yours. No, so he doesn't whistle up the tanks? Impossible! Impossible! And sovereignty, too! Incredible! No, no, why on earth should I? Yes, yes, I'm taking it down. Don't you worry; I'm an old underground hand. Eh, what did you say? Ah, OK, OK, OK. Everything will be OK. Mm-hmm. I'll ring Himself this evening. Around ten OK? . . . Isn't that on the late side? Ah, the Japanese thing. No, if it's *Madame Butterfly* it'll be earlier than *Turandot*. Yes, if worse comes to worst, direct to his box. The number? I've got it. The most important thing is, let the ambassador know; he's a bit of a loose cannon. Well, all right then, thanks. It'll all be OK. Mm-hmm. All the best. OK, OK. [*Hangs up.*] OK, Gustav Adolfovich, cut me a slice of that watermelon, eh, [*Pause.*] Well then, Gentlemen Ministers. [*At this word, everybody gives a start.*] I have an important announcement to make. Democracy has been established here.

[*General stupefaction.*]

Meaning?

What do you mean?

Established, how?

What sort of democracy? Socialist? Peoples'?

A new kind?

Western?

Athenian?

Everything's foreign.

When are we going to learn to use nouns without adjectives?

That depends on what the noun is. All right, all right. Don't get too smart, will you? What's happened then, Basil Modestovich?

Nothing, really, Petrovich. That Georgian, you know, that foreign minister of theirs, says that half an hour ago, Himself announced at a press conference that democracy is being introduced here. [*Shouts.*] Matilda! [*Enter Matilda.*] Matilda, no calls. Until further notice.

What if it's Them?

Them? All right, but only if it's Himself. Got that?

Yes. Comrade Gensec?

Or the Commander-in-Chief. Is that clear?

Yes, Comrade Gensec.

And don't call me Gensec any more. Got that? You can say President.

Yes, Comrade President.

Better leave out the Comrade. Sounds a bit weird. Better just

Mister. Understood?

Yes, Mister Gensec. I mean, Comrade President, er, Comrade Gensec. Er, Mister President, I mean.

That's better.

[*Exit Matilda, unbuttoning her blouse.*]

What on earth is going to happen now, Basil Modestovich?

Now don't you worry, Cecilia. It'll be all right.

All right! Here you are, president already, what about us?

Aren't we being a little hasty, Basil Modestovich?

No, no, on the contrary, Petrovich. The press will be here in half an hour. We've got to be ready. Of course, Himself can blurt out what he likes, but where they go, we go. After all, we've got a common border, not to mention ideals.

Not to mention culture. Starting with the Minister.

Why, how dare you, Gustav Adolfovich!

So you're a Mister Minister now, Petrovich. Not to mention Gustav. And you, Cecilia?

I am Ms Minister?

Why on earth not, Cecilia?

Well, it sounds, somehow, like . . . neither fish nor fowl. Doesn't go well with a skirt. I wear a skirt, after all.

We had noticed.

You'll get used to it: Cecilia . . . was there something between you two?

What are you referring to, Basil Modestovich?

This Georgian Wogachov!

Really, Basil Modestovich! How could you think such a thing!

You're blushing, Cecilia. And you used to be with the Bolshoi!

Democracy

What would Stanislavsky say? And what are those daily milk baths for . . . What could you have seen in him? Oh, I know, those Politburo big shots. Spheres of influence [*swings his hips*] and all that—the Marilyn Munroe doctrine.

He is a Georgian, don't forget, Basil Modestovich. Their—

Shut up, Petrovich!

—thing: stick it in a bucket and the water boils.

Petrovich!

Ah, Cecilia, Cecilia. Still hot, aren't you. On the other hand, of course, who are we? The declining West. All right, stop blushing. You're reminding me of the old banner—not to mention the curtain. Right then, Gustav Adolfovich, what did we produce here before?

Before what?

Before the Change for the Better. Before historical materialism and industrialization.

Ah, before 1945. Bacon, Basil Modestovich. We supplied all England with bacon.

Well, England's got piles of bacon of its own nowadays.

Smoked eels. We supplied all of Europe with smoked eels. Even Italy. An Italian poet even wrote these lines: '*Eel, siren/Of the Baltic Sea . . .*' There was a huge cannery. Produced sixteen varieties of eel.

Aha, the French too have this dish: eel bourgignon. All you need is red wine.

Sure. Since it's fish.

On the whole, fish goes with white.

Now they're telling me how to cook! It takes three days to make this snake dry. You get a hammer and nail the thing to the wall, straight through the gills. To dry it out.

Smoke it, you mean?

Oh, no! This is just so it stops coiling. They are just too stubborn—eels, I mean. Durable is the word. Even after three days it coils. Even when sliced and in the pot. Still darts and dodges—

Like at an interrogation.

—even in the pot. Twirls and wiggles. Because it's so slippery. So you lace it with some red.

Like I said: fish. No blood in it. Make the thing bleed, and the dodging's over.

That's why they quit catching them, I guess. Can't afford burgundy for everyone.

Besides, sets a bad example. Excessive resistance, etcetera. Smacks of a national symbol. More exactly—an ideal. Cut and slice me, so to speak, I won't budge.

Cold-blooded, that's why.

Like I said. The result is aberrant behaviour. As is often the case with ideals. Us, we've got five litres of red, and it's all hot. While an ideal is always on the cold side. Hence: incompatability.

Of the hot with the cold?

The real with the ideal?

No, materialism with idealism.

Ah, a deadly mix.

No, just blood-letting.

Bloodshed, in our tongue.

To cool them off.

Yeah, the hotheads.

Or else to redden ideals somewhat.

Right, to give them a human face.

Sort of. To reduce tension. This way they are better preserved.

Who?

Ideals. In a cell, especially.

In a word, canned products.

Uh-huh. In their own juices. Especially when you regain consciousness—

Macabre.

—on your bunk, coiling. In every sense, an eel. The only catch: no good for export.

Macabre.

How many brands did you say we used to produce, Gustav Adolfovich?

Sixteen. The cannery was producing sixteen sorts of eel. Smoked, marinated, in olive oil, etcetera. In its own juices, too.

And now?

Now? Alarm clocks and radios now. Good alarm clocks, mind you. With the Orthodox chiming. As for radios, only medium- and long-wave. As for short-wave, this guy [*nods to Petrovich*] outlawed them.

That's the kind of sea we've got, Basil Modestovich. Of the tin-can shade, anyway. Some correspondence, I reckon, is in order.

So all that's left of our eel is waves. And long ones at that.

Right. Won't do as an export item. Nor will the alarm clocks, with all that tin and Orthodox chiming. That particular brand is in short supply in the West, that's the rub. Not to mention demand. Should we ship them to Himself, then, eh? Though that, of course, is no export. Or even import.

More like metabolism, if [*nods in the bear's direction*] not exile.

Guuuuuustav!

OK, OK Petrovich. As Wogochvili puts it, okay. Siberia needs alarm clocks, too.

That's how the guards wake up!

OK, OK. So what else did we used to have, Gustav?

Cheese with caraway seeds. Amber necklaces. It was just an agrarian country. Farmsteads everywhere. There was trade in pigskin as well. Good quality. Napoleon used to order his buckskins only from us.

Is that it?

That's the lot.

Minerals?

You know very well. Just peat . . . Come to think of it, what made them all so keen to conquer us anyhow? Now Germans, now you people . . . A fat lot you all got out of it.

That's not the right way to argue, Gustav Adolfovich. Dangerous, even—isn't that so, Petrovich?

Mm-hmm. People used to get put away for much less.

Well, there's no time to argue about that. Not to mention being put away. The press will be here in half an hour . . . Right, then. We are going to restore the agricultural might of the nation. Europe can breathe easy: eels fresh and smoked will be in full spate. Bacon and cheese will flood East. Even to Siberia. Hide to the highest bidder. Eels to be a state monopoly, the rest entrepreneurial, whatever that means. We will consider the question of foreign investment and concessions. Our hand will be stretched out in friendship to our brothers overseas. We will abolish censorship, permit the Church and trade unions. Is that all? Eh?

Free elections, no doubt.

And free elections. Without free elections, no foreign investment.

Removal of allied troops?

Or failing that . . . out of sight like our own ears. Democracy's in means tanks are out. And vice versa. I'll ring Himself this evening and ask him.

But this is a 180 degree turn! For this sort of thing people used to . . .

Ah, make it an even 360! What's the matter, Petrovich? Do you want to go back to Ryazan? The press is going to be here in half an hour, gentlemen ministers. Don't you see? They hounded Himself to the point that he decreed democracy here. What will we have left to decree if we get hounded too? Invite back some descendant of Wittold the Great and put him on the throne? It's even easier for us, actually; we don't have to pull our armed forces out of anywhere, right? Let's get going and extend conscription into the army. National pride is boosted, plus the number of mouths to feed gets slashed by half. Not to mention heads at demonstrations. It really is easier for you, Petrovich. Am I right, Gustav Adolfovich? Anyway, who is for?

And what about minorities?

[*Suspiciously*] Whom do you have in mind?

It's obvious, whom [*nods towards the bear*].

Basil Modestovich! He means us!

Take it easy, Petrovich. After all, he's looking out for himself, too. A kraut's a kraut, Eastern or not. Isn't that so, Gustav?

Ja.

Zonderkomand!

Becher is too.

Still, he was taken prisoner. And in '41 besides.

I gave myself up.

Sure, in '45.

Zonderkomand.

Actually, Waffen SS. Totenkopf Division.

Who sticks to the bygones gets his eye poked out.

And who forgets that—both. Totenkopf, indeed.

Becher is too. And yet he's foreign minister.

That's precisely why. A foreign minister must be a foreigner. That's only logical. Isn't that so, Gustav?

Natürlich—that is, of course.

Ah, our ministers are all foreigners. Save Public Health. Though he is a sweetie.

[*Angrily*] Cecilia! Oh, well, we'll get to this later. No time for that now. Neither for minorities. Besides, foreign aid is not contingent on them. In a word, Gustav, are you for or against?

I'm for, I'm for. I always thought loans and concessions were the way out. Loans especially. Why are you looking like that, Petrovich? You said yourself we needed foreign currency!

What way out? Out of what? You're just a left-over contra, Gustav. 'Finance minister' as well! Just remember Poland. Loans have to be repaid, and with interest. Why do you think a capitalist gives you loans—to breed eels with? Nuts! It's to drive you into debt. A debtor is just his cup of tea, the bee's knees. Especially if it's a whole country. That's why it's called capitalism, because capital gets borrowed. If it weren't for debt, there'd be no capitalism.

Sure. We haven't borrowed from them in fifty years and they're still there. It's us who soon won't be here.

That's because we're on our own. The socialist camp. That's why they don't like us; we don't borrow. We undermine business. And the longer there are people like us . . .

Oh yes! We've read about it. Liberation movements and so forth. So let's be in debt. Anything's better than an empty belly. I mean for the populace.

You're an unprincipled opportunist, Gustav! Agrarian. The earth breathes through you. Kulak's semen. Nationalist.

Just watch your tongue, Petrovich. The populace has nothing to munch on, I'm telling you. It's easy to stick to principles individually. You can dig your heels in and not accept loans. With your rations especially. But those without rations, how about them? You get to feeling sorry for them. Not you, of course. You don't care, just like Old Bandylegs there [*nods towards the bear*]. Meanwhile, we've got zero population growth. Who can multiply on cucumbers and boiled cabbage? Now even the fish have all gone to Sweden. No, loans are better than this, any day.

Basil Modestovich, you hear that? He's insulting an allied power [*nods towards the bear*]! Finance minister, and can't understand why a capitalist invests in a socialist country!

They invest, Petrovich, because our labour is reliable. No strikes, for instance, like they have. For them, investing in us is like marrying a widow. No risk. Becher used to tell me a bank that invests in a socialist country looks more solid. Its balance sheets look better. Hence, more respect, more trust, more clients. As for the fish, they have all truly gone to Sweden. Indeed, I complained to Himself and he promised to send a submarine over there to sort things out. No results so far. On the other hand, he's gone in for loans as well. As they go, we go, Petrovich. A common border, after all. Never mind how many degrees you turn. Anyway, who's for?

There's only four of us, Basil Modestovich. Twenty-two ministers are missing. The Council of Ministers . . .

Council of Ministers! Council of Ministers! You'll be saying 'Politburo' next, Gustav. It's terrific luck they're not here; Stalin himself couldn't have coped with a crowd like that in half an hour. Her moron—the Public Health stud—alone takes an eternity. Twenty-two are missing, he says! It's the other way around: even we are too many for a democracy! What if the votes split equally, even if I have the casting vote?

I can leave if you wish, Basil Modestovich.

Stay where you are, Cecilia. There's only one way out. Vote unanimously. We are the nerve centre of the state—ministers of finance, interior, culture and me. Wait a minute, though! Would it be better if one were against? Otherwise it isn't a democracy. Gustav, do you want to be against? No, Finance is too serious. What

215

about you, Petrovich?

So I'm not serious. Internal Affairs and Justice.

Sorry, I wasn't thinking. Cecilia? Although, the Minister of Culture in opposition—looks bad. Then . . . then . . . I'll do it! Even better. 'The Gensec complies under pressure from his ministers . . .'

But you're not 'The Gensec' any more! You just renamed yourself . . .

Better and better! The President complies under pressure from his ministers . . . Sounds like a democracy. Majority and minority.

Some democracy! More like a revolution from above! Especially if twenty-two ministers are missing. People used to be . . .

Petro-o-vich! The press will be here in half an hour! Good Lord, Petrovich! That's what democracy is, a revolution from above. A palace coup. In our circumstances, anyway. A revolution from below is what? Dictatorship of the proletariat. Is that what you want? In half an hour, if we don't agree, you're going to get it. Think of yourself, at least, if you don't care about me. Not to mention Gustav and Cecilia.

You mean you care about me, Basil Modestovich?

About us all, Petrovich. We are the brain of the state.

Nerve-centre, rather.

Nerve-centre, then. Who's going to worry about *that*? The body, you think? A body can't worry about a brain, can it? The point is that the rest is the body; we're the brain. The brain is that which receives the signal first, democracy or not democracy. Who should be gorging on grouse and watermelon? The brain, of course! Because there isn't enough grouse and watermelon for everybody. You can't fill thirty bellies with one watermelon. Not to mention a grouse. Four—yes. Same with history.

Theoretically, you could divide a watermelon in thirty. It would be unequal, perhaps, but possible.

Somehow I missed the part where you divided anything into thirty parts, Gustav, equal or unequal. A-a-ah! We're wasting time! History is being made here. In the brain! Are we voting, or not?

What's the point of voting if you've decided everything?

Yes, if the revolution is taking place in your brain?

Has taken place, I'd say.

It's not interesting, voting for the sake of appearances.

Yes, we've done that before.

What sort of democracy do you call this?

Especially if you're against it?

Better if we're unanimous.

Or let us be three against and you for.

Yes, that's less bother.

It's not democracy, though.

Mm-hmm. Tyranny.

But less bother.

Come to think of it, Basil Modestovich, what if they've set all this up specially?

Set what up?

Well, this 180 degree turn. So they can overrun us again afterwards.

History repeats itself, Marx said.

Yes, it's all a hoax.

That's why they're taking their troops out.

So it's better if we're in opposition, then.

You can't trust them.

Otherwise it will look as if we're not loyal.

And you will be.

We'll be for it, and you'll come up smelling like a rose.

So tyranny would be better.

Even if it is left-wing.

Because if you're called East, you'll be pensioned off, but where will we be?

Clicking on an abacus.

Running a personnel department.

Translating articles on manure.

In Ulan-Bator.

Or Karaganda.

That's if we're lucky.

Yesus Maria! Yesus Maria! And this is the nation's brain! The press will be here in twenty minutes, for heaven's sake! If we don't take a vote, you'll find yourself in Karaganda the day after tomorrow. Well, in a week, anyway. Because if it's a tyranny, even a leftist one, the press will go mad. If the press goes mad, Himself goes mad. Even if he doesn't, it will look as if he's encouraging tyranny. Or their ambassador will go mad and send for the tanks. And all of us will be swept away to hell and gone—with the support of the masses. That'll be Eisenstein all right. Has it got through to you yet?

[*Pause.*]

It's getting there, Basil Modestovich.

Exactly, Petrovich. And let me be in the minority and against. What sort of a democracy is it without an opposition? So I'll be the opposition. Loyal, of course, because an opposition can't be trusted, whereas I can. I mean, since I trust myself. That is, at the head of the opposition there should stand a man whom you would trust as yourself. To control it. But there is no such person. I wouldn't even appoint my old woman.

Aha, the opposition is just like a woman. You might trust her, but you can't control her.

Or trust her. There is no man or woman you can trust. Only I am that man. Therefore I must be the opposition. Is it getting through?

It is.

It already has.

Almost.

I'm the minority. You're the majority. I give way to you. That's what democracy is—when the minority gives way.

I thought it was when the majority and the minority have equal rights.

No, it's when the tanks get pulled out.

Or when the minority becomes the majority.

As a consequence of voting.

Uh-huh. And vice versa.

You mean when the minority submits to the majority.

Or the other way around. As in our case.

What sort of minority is Basil Modestovich really? Majority, that's what he is!

I think it's the other way around. Objectively he is, but subjectively, no.

I object: the point is, who's the subject?

Since the object is obvious.

Well, that's what voting is for, to sort out the objective from the subjective.

And what if it turns out that he's the minority and we're the majority?

Then thank your lucky stars, Cecilia.

And if it's the other way around?

Subjectivity triumphs.

And what if it's unanimous?

Then we vote again. Right, Basil Modestovich?

Uh-huh. Only, let's get a move on!

Even if he ends up being the minority?

Ah, cut the sentimentality, Cecilia!

No, really. It's awkward . . .

If worse comes to worst, Cecilia, picture it like this: he's a minority which cares about the majority.

All of us, not just himself.

Including you.

I still don't like it. Because Basil Modestovich ends up as some sort of menshevik.

We keep telling you, Cecilia. It's not 1917.

That's right. Not to mention that in 1917, it was the majority taking care of the minority.

More precisely, the bolsheviks defeated the mensheviks.

What do you mean, more precisely? What do you mean by that, Gustav?

That the victory of the majority and the victory of the bolsheviks over the mensheviks are not the same thing. Precisely the opposite, actually. Percentage-wise, at any rate. Relative to the nation, the bolsheviks were a vanishingly small minority.

Well, now he's piped up! Basil Modestovich, you hear this rubbish of Gustav's? For that sort of thing in the old days . . . Where's my brief case?

Ah, leave him be, Petrovich. There's only fifteen minutes left. So, ministers. Do we vote?

Well, really, Basil Modestovich! It's blatant counter-revolution! He should be grabbed!

He can't be grabbed, Petrovich: we need him to make a quorum. Since three for, one against, is victory for the majority. Two against one—just a brawl. Without Gustav it wouldn't be a vote, it'd be God knows what. Disgrace in the eyes of world public opinion. First we have to vote, I tell you.

And after? Afterwards we can grab him, yes?

Afterwards, Petrovich—if the majority wins—there'll be no reason to grab Gustav. Because afterwards there will be democracy. What was counter-revolution before democracy, under it becomes a heroic record.

Then I am against democracy, Basil Modestovich. For whom shall I be grabbing under it? Myself, maybe?

That's precisely why you should vote 'for'. Under democracy— don't you worry. There's always room for that. Lots of people are going to be against, in opposition. Why, you can start with me. Although I'm loyal opposition.

Oh, how can you talk like that, Basil Modestovich? For me to . . .

It'll be easier for you, Petrovich. Under democracy, I mean. Less work. First off you release all those who are for democracy. That'll take you a few years. Then you grab those who are against, that's really a piece of cake. The old guard and so on—well, you know them better than me.

All the same, I'm against. Because those who get released will rush to the palace, and it's curtains for us.

That's the very reason you should vote 'for'. Why should they rush in if we're 'for'? For the same thing as they are? If, right here in the palace, the minority submits to the majority, eh? That's their golden dream. Besides, don't go letting them out all at once. One at a time.

They'll push their way in. Demonstrations, in a word. From the root, 'demon'.

I thought it came from 'monster'.

'*Demos*', Cecilia, '*demos*'. 'The people', in our language.

It doesn't matter, their golden dream is universal justice. As far as justice is concerned, they're unanimous.

Because they're ignorant, Petrovich. Because they've been in opposition for too long. And we—we'll explain everything to them, won't we Cecilia? Shall we entrust that task to the Ministry of Culture?

I'm taking it down, Basil Modestovich.

It's being taken down in any case, Cecilia [*nods to the bear*]. Not now. There's no time. Well, anyway, toss them that idea, unanimity is the mother of dictatorship.

The child, actually.

The child always takes after the mother. The main thing is that they understand that what they fought for is what they've got. The goal has been reached, as the Kaiser said. There's no one to fight with any longer. Not us, at any rate.

Yeah, but what about justice?

Yes, they're for the triumph of justice. For ideals.

Exactly. They're against us. We're the government.

When we vote, they're going to be for us. The triumph of justice, Gustav, is expressed in the same forms as the triumph of injustice. I mean the result is the same: a government.

Oi, I should make a note of that.

Yeah, give Teddy [*nods to the bear*] a break. He's been sweating and toiling for much too long . . .

[*Enter Matilda, clad only in a camisole and bloomers.*] Mister President, the press has assembled out there. They're asking for you.

Tell them the lunch break isn't over yet. Understand?

Yes, Mister President. Oi, is it true we're going to have a

democracy?

Wait and see. In fifteen minutes. Your wages will remain the same, at any rate. Working hours and telephone likewise. Off you go. [*Exit Matilda, tearing off her camisole.*]

What's with her?

How do you mean, Petrovich?

Well, her . . . that she's dressed so, er, lightly. Isn't it a bit early in the year for that?

Could be because of the bodyguard. Some monkey business.

Getting jealous, Cecilia?

How could you say such a thing, Basil Modestovich!

Or else she's symbolizing the condition of our economy.

Or the departure from dogma.

Most likely the latter.

After all, she represents the people.

Yes, the working class.

But not the proletariat.

Peasants, then.

Right. Healthy looks. Like the proverb says: blood and milk.

Or—the intelligentsia.

[*Explodes.*] Some intelligentsia! Ooooh, shameless bitch! In the old days even hard currency bars were off limits to her kind! What's she got? No foreign languages to speak of. Only ours and the local. Intelligentsia! I offered her a free ticket to *Swan Lake* the other day, and what do you think? She wouldn't go! I'd show her . . . I'd have her . . . She hasn't even read Turgenev. Tur-ge-nev!

Jealousy, Cecilia. Stark, scientific jealousy. Matilda's been in the Party since she was eighteen. Daughter of very trusted comrades. Not to mention Becher's niece. And as for *Swan Lake*, she was working overtime that week. Preparing my agricultural policy paper for the Congress.

Like I said, blood-cum-milk.

Swan song, anyway. For agriculture, I mean.

Tchaikovsky, in a word.

Saint-Saens!

Good for you, Cecilia.

Saint-Saens is no match for Tchaikovsky, no way! What do the frogs know of collective farms?

With frogs, Petrovich, the main thing was the neck.

With swans.

[*Bluntly*] Legs. You can check that with Cecilia.

Well, gentlemen, are we voting or not?

Yes, let's vote.

And will our salary stay the same, Basil Modestovich?

Yes. It's a risky line of work, after all.

Hazardous occupation.

For this sort of thing you get milk rations *gratis* in an atomic power station.

Oh, I imagine our diet won't change much. We're not going to leave the Warsaw Pact and Comecon. And Himself has always maintained that there should be a common menu for all the allies. A pledge, so to speak, of mutual understanding.

That's right. Digestion as common denominator.

Actually, digestion's end result.

Gustav! Ladies present!

Well, as to your salary, that you have to ask Gustav. Milk? I wouldn't recommend the milk. The cows are local after all. Their udders drive Geiger counters wilder than the reactor does. Isn't that so, Petrovich?

Yes. Giving that milk for danger payment is an absolute tautology.

Unless Himself joins the Common Market, that is. I wish he would, of course; as it is they've got no soap over there.

And what's the point of knocking the brains about with the five-year plan all the time? They'd do it for him in Brussels. Their computers are better anyway, at least sturdier.

That's it, he warbled something about a common European home.

On the other hand, in Eurasia they only take a bath once a month. Ask Cecilia, she remembers. Or better still, Petrovich.

Just you be quiet, Gustav! Whatever soap you used wouldn't wash off the contra stain.

There he goes, the voice of the patriot. You're homesick for that Ryazan of yours, Petrovich. *Nostalgie de la boue.* No other words for it. All these years here and still hankering after the pigsty. Though you did marry a local.

You leave my old woman out of this, Gustav. Though she may be local, she's of mixed blood. With the local goods you couldn't find a clitoris if you used a lamp in daylight. Cold fish!

Petrovich! Ladies present!

That's why the men here are such benders. Or demonstrators. It's hard to decide which book to throw at them.

Basil Modestovich, he's insulting our national dignity.

Ministers! Ministers! No quarrelling.

I always thought a foreigner should not be minister of the interior. Foreign minister, yes. Home affairs, no.

You're a dyed in the wool contra, Gustav. Not to mention that the clitoris is an internal matter. Still, how would you know, with your native squaw?

Why, how dare you!

For shame, Petrovich!

Gentlemen, no quarrelling!

Shame is unknown to the minister of the interior, Cecilia. The minister of the interior is like a gynaecologist.

I always said a foreigner oughtn't . . .

Gentlemen ministers, gentlemen ministers, do calm yourselves. In the first place, Gustav, you're wrong. The minister of the interior—

and justice!

—the minister of the interior and justice must be a foreigner. It guarantees greater objectivity, and no nepotism. Remember Roman Law. Then again, it's always better if an oppressor—and the law is always an oppressor—is a foreigner. Better to curse a foreigner than your own countryman. That's what makes empires tick. Remember the Caesars or, worse comes to worst, Stalin. It's a kind of psychotherapy. It's healthier to hate a stranger than your own.

Oi, I must make a note of that.

But I can't vote alongside a man who insults the dignity of my nation!

Had he been one of our own, then, no, you couldn't, Gustav. But as he's a foreigner, you can. Because he's acting naturally. Moreover, thanks to his being natural, you're acting naturally too in getting mad. Which is the natural reaction. That's the first thing. Secondly, his gynaecological observations, though they do insult the dignity of the nation, address only half of it. And even Cecilia over there isn't reacting.

What's it to her? She's got four children. Broad cheek-bones and all that.

Or because she knows that Petrovich is exaggerating. Or, rather, minimizing.

He lost his temper, Basil Modestovich.

Did you, Petrovich?

Mm-hmm.

In any case, the dignity of a nation is not defined by the dimensions of this thing. And in any event, we must be solicitous of the dignity of the whole nation. Therefore let us add to our referendum the restoration of the flag and the national anthem from before the Change for the Better, eh? How does that strike you, Petrovich?

Well, as for me, I'm for it. Although I could never figure out what it stood for. Not even under torture.

Now then, Cecilia, your department.

Grey stripes on a white field. Symbolizes the local climate. Weather in general.

Like TV interference.

And I always traced it to the Old Glory.

I, to a calico. Yellow stars, there, though.

So, then, we restore the colours of the National Weather. Anthem?

The anthem, Basil Modestovich, was no great shakes. You could sing it to the tune of '*La Cucaracha*' or 'My Darling Clementine'. Like '*Deutschland, Deutschland, über alles*'.

N-yes, Himself might wince at that.

Mightn't understand it.

Might take it the wrong way.

Perhaps we could adapt theirs.

Let's not get carried away.

Only five more minutes.

How about Brubeck's 'Take Five'? Cool, yet energetic.

He's still alive; there'd be royalties. The reserves wouldn't stand for it.

How about something folkish?

'Tears of the Fisher Girl'?

Dreary.

'Where's My Laddie'?

Himself may not take to that.

Since Laddie's obviously in Siberia.

Maybe 'Dear Land, I'll Never Part from You'.

That's better.

Much better.

Folk—both the tune and the lyrics.

No ideology.

I always sing that to the tune of Sidney Bechet's '*Petite Fleur*'.

Come on then, let's here here it.

[*Cecilia sings.*] '*Dear land, I'll never part from you/I'll never leave you for any reason.*' Oi, I'm not in voice today.

Not bad, not bad.

Not bad at all.

So, shall we vote, gentlemen ministers? [*Hums.*] Dear land, I'll never part from you, pom-pom-pom-pom-pom-pom-pom, pom-pom-pom-pom-pom-pom.

Let's vote, let's vote.

Historical moment.

Great—pom-pom-pom-pom-pom-pom—event.

One hundred eighty degree turn.

Democracy.

The wolves are fed and the sheep are safe.

Both the wolves and the sheep.

Pom-pom-pom-pom-pom-pom, pom-pom-pom-pom-pom-pom.

Those for, raise your hands.

Why bother? We know anyway.

Because [*nods to the bear*] it's being recorded. And on video. Maybe Himself is watching live. No, he's at a press conference.

Oh, that's probably finished.

He's finished and we're just starting. In two minutes' time. Well, who's for?

[*They vote.*]

So, three for. Who's against? [*Raises his hand.*] One against. By a majority of votes—pom-pom-pom-pom-pom-pom—ugh, can't get it out of my head . . .

Basil Modestovich, it's the national anthem!

Ah, yes, sorry . . . The resolution on the transfer to a democratic form of rule and economic reform—pom-pom-pom-phew!— carried. Signatures. [*Signs.*] Gustav. [*Holds out the sheet, Gustav signs.*] Petrovich [*Holds out the sheet, Petrovich signs.*] Pass it on to Cecilia. [*Petrovich passes it over, Cecilia signs.*] Hey, Matilda!

[*Enter Matilda, stark naked.*]

Translate this into our language.

When?

Now.

Oi, the press is out there.

They can wait. Lunch break isn't over yet.

But they're pushing down the doors.

Who cares? It's not 1917. You translate. And—what's this

masquerade of yours for? Or, rather, vice versa?

There's been a 180 degree turn.

That's 180, Matilda. And you've gone all 360.

This is to symbolize irreversibility, Mister President. That after democracy there is nothing else. And that democracy is natural.

The press is going to love it. A good shot: you standing next to our honey-lover [*nods to the bear*]. Go translate.

Oi, straight away. [*Runs off.*]

Petrovich, want a cigar? Fidel sent them.

Uh-huh. Like I said, blood and milk.

Here are the matches . . . Well, as to milk we are fully informed: Geiger goes beserk.

As to blood also.

True enough. About blood, we've got no questions either.

What I wonder is, what is it that makes Matilda so keen on democracy, milk or blood?

Both. Since she knows nothing about either. . . Cigar, Gustav? Ah, but I am going senile: you quit. As for you, Cecilia, finish off the watermelon.

Yeah, God knows now when we'll get another shipment.

Soon, except that it'll be from Germany.

Or the States.

Most likely Germany, as part of the foreign aid.

No watermelons, though. They don't grow there.

Yeah. They too may pay the price for geographical advantage.

It'll come, Gustav, don't worry. Himself will see to that.

Yes, after all, this is a highly symbolic fruit.

Vegetable.

Who cares? Main thing, green on the outside, red inside.

The colours of hope and passion.

Not to mention shed blood.

Same thing anyway.

The only catch: it's hard to tell whether it's ripe or not—until you carve it up, that is.

And on top of that it has seeds.

Big deal, seeds! You can always spit them out.

True enough.

On second thoughts I'd like to have a cigar, in honour of the occasion.

What occasion?

Well, it is democracy, after all.

With Gustav it's surely blood.

I for one wouldn't resume the habit for democracy. For blood's sake especially.

And for what would you?

For nothing, Gustav. Mind you, I've never kicked it. Besides, Fidel keeps sending the stuff. To me, that is. To Himself he's stopped.

It's easy for him. All he's got is an island.

Right. Only ideals to share. He can afford not to shave [*a nod, to the portraits*].

[*They smoke a while.*]

Listen, Petrovich, which do you like better, the past or the future?

I don't know Basil Modestovich. I never thought of that. I would have said the future before, I guess; now, the past. I am Internal Affairs, after all.

And you, Gustav?

It depends. Sometimes the future, sometimes the past.

The present, then. You, Cecilia, I don't ask. With you it's clear. Hope and passion non-stop.

A woman, Basil Modestovich, is always more interested in the future. Maternal instincts, after all.

Don't be so complex, Cecilia. What's 'maternal' got to do with it? Just plain instincts.

What a rude man you are, Petrovich!

If I am rude, it's only because I'd hate to be studying German in my old age. Or English. Isn't that right, Basil Modestovich?

True enough.

And what about yourself, Basil Modestovich? Which do you like best?

No idea, Petrovich. In the end, I suppose, the past. Because it's in the majority.

This reminds me, Basil Modestovich: what if they ask who authorized this? No parliament, nobody . . .

They won't. It'll never enter their heads.

Still.

Say history.

They're persistent, though. Troublesome and persistent.

So?

Just because of one telephone call . . .

The telephone, Cecilia, is an instrument of history. Personal history, at any rate. Sometimes national. Especially when it's recorded. Then you can't differentiate the personal and the personnel. So, then, you can tell them, history. Or say, revolution. For them it's the same thing.

But they'll say, where are the masses, the gunfire, the barricades?

You tell them this ain't a movie. That revolution always catches the people unawares. And if they're so keen to see bloodshed, I can call in the troops and open fire on them. Pests!

Oi!

No need for that. They won't ask. Which reminds me Petrovich: phone Becher in Japan please. Tell him not to worry when he sees the papers tomorrow—especially naked Matilda. Otherwise for all we know he might panic and ask for political asylum and set up a government in exile.

Yes, he's a man of the old school. Pity he wasn't here today.

Mm-hmm, indeed. The grouse was marvellous, not to mention the gravy. Coffee?

Translated from the Russian by Alan Myer

MINERVA
PAPERBACKS AVAILABLE NOW

BLEEDING SINNERS
MOY McCRORY

"Generous and compassionate, and to coin a
phrase, bloody marvellous"
Irish Times
£3.99

ABBA ABBA
ANTHONY BURGESS

"Scholarship and imagination blend together
here to produce an intensely literary book
that reads as if it were a period document"
Anthony Curtis, *Financial Times*
£3.99

THE SURPRISE OF
BURNING
MICHAEL DOANE

"As sophisticated and achieved an exercise in
point of view and narrative consciousness as
anything in recent years. Its images,
negative and positive, are almost chemically

TLS
£4.50

JONATHAN RABAN
NEW WORLD

There was a cardinal in the dogwood tree, just six feet away from where I was sitting in my rocker. The bird was blinded to me by the mosquito-mesh wall of the verandah. I didn't move a muscle. Against the flurry of white petals, the cardinal's crimson feathers were like a holy wounding, a splash of fresh blood on a laundered sheet. Its head swivelled to exhibit its horned crest, combed and oiled to a fine point. A skirl of wind rattled the map of Guntersville on my knee, the chains of the rocker creaked in their ring-bolts—and the cardinal rocketed out of the blossom in a flaming streak of red.

Things happened fast in this town; a lot faster than they happened in Manhattan. I'd crossed the bridge to Guntersville, Alabama, a little after ten in the morning; by four in the afternoon I had assembled the materials of a complete new life. I was a resident of Polecat Hollow, with a two-bedroom cinderblock cabin in the woods at the edge of the water. My telephone was connected. I had a box number at the Post Office; I had engaged a once-a-week maid, stacked the Frigidaire with a sackful of groceries, ordered a typewriter so that I could be a useful and productive citizen.

That freedom to move—the hallmark of being an American—entailed a corresponding freedom to settle. My demand for instant membership of the community was met without a glimmer of surprise. Footslogging around the realtors, I picked up the low-down on the local bars and restaurants, accumulated a deck of business cards with people's home numbers scribbled at the top ('Just call *any* time') was invited to a party and was introduced to the elaborate network of cousinship in which a few related families appeared to have the town's affairs sewn up. Posted from uncle to wife's brother-in-law, to father, to nephew, to wife's mother and on to wife's mother's sister-in-law, I felt I'd strayed into some great tribal house on the Arabian Gulf. The Lusks, Neelys, Alreds, Smiths and Willises had coagulated into something like the Al-Thanis or the Al-Makhtoums. Walking past the hilly, well-tended graveyard on O'Brig Avenue, I noticed that the names on the tombstones of a hundred years ago still worked as a reasonably efficient business directory for Guntersville in 1989, and that even the longest-dead were still honoured with tributes of cut flowers.

It had taken half a dozen meetings, a few telephone calls and a windy promenade around the town to find my cabin in the woods. At 250 dollars a month, it was reckoned to be discouragingly expensive by Marshall County standards; I decided not to let on what I'd paid for my shoe-box on East 18th.

The Hedgepeth place was a summer-house; it was gloomy, cold and smelled of damp and desertion. A souvenir tea-cloth showing a map of Puerto Rico was the main ornament to the living-room, while the ceiling of the main bedroom had been tiled with squares of tarnished mirror-glass. When I lay on the bed I was appalled to find myself staring at the body of a bald man, his image broken up Cubist-fashion into a grid of angled planes. Who on earth could bear to wake to the sight of their own nakedness so splayed and deranged? Guntersville people, apparently.

It took me a while to notice the ants. Unpacking my sponge-bag in the bathroom, I thought I saw the brown shagpile carpet ripple like a cornfield in a wind. Looking closer, I saw a colony of ants the size of wasps out on some kind of jungle exercise in the woolly undergrowth. When I flushed the cistern, a hundred or so ant-marines tumbled into the toilet-bowl from their positions under the rim.

I drove the Spirit back into town, a mile away, and consulted my new friend William, the pharmacist.

'They black ants? Or are they a kind of reddy-brown?'

'Black—I think.'

'I *hope* it's black ants you got out there. If they're a *brown* ant, it could be you got *fire ants* on your place. Then you got problems.' He was searching round among his poisons. 'Friend of mine, he had fire ants once . . . he just went out into his backyard one morning . . . end of the day, his daughter came home, found him laying there *dayud*. Fire ants. Yes—he was killed by the fire ants,' he said with a soft twinkle. 'That was a misfortunate man.'

As he spoke, my ants started changing colour rapidly from black to brown.

'But if they're inside your house, they'll most likely be black ants, I hope so, anyway; I wouldn't like to think of you with fire ants in your house. How big you say they are?'

I found it hard to control the trembling of my forefinger and thumb.

William nodded and smiled; he looked significantly pleased by what I'd shown him.

'Oh, yes, we do get them real big around here—'

Before I left the drugstore with two bottles of sweet antbane, he asked me if I knew about brown recluse spiders. They were worse than fire ants; far worse. There was probably a brown recluse somewhere out at my place; most people had them, without knowing. They were no bigger than William's thumb-nail. They didn't spin give-away webs. They just hid and waited to get you. If you left a pair of boots in a closet, a brown recluse might well take up residence in a toe. If there was some rotten wood in your porch, or up in the rafters . . . The brown recluse was the duke of the dark corners of Alabama. William knew a lot of people who'd died, or been permanently paralysed, after being bitten by a brown recluse.

'Why, the Reverend Billy Graham—*he* was bitten by a brown recluse. He got treatment, but that's why he still walks so stiff. That was a brown recluse spider.'

Back at the cabin, I moved as cautiously as if I was burgling it, examining each patch of carpet before I dared to plant a foot there. But there was no question: my ants were coal-black; not deadly, just a nuisance to be got rid of. Following the instructions on the bottle, I booby-trapped the house with half-inch rectangles of white card, then shook out on each card a couple of drops of the poisonous clear syrup. Within a quarter of an hour the ants were assembled round the cards like so many guests at an all-male black-tie dinner. I watched over them with an odd, hostly feeling of benevolence. Poisoners, I remembered, tend to have milk and water manners— like Dr Crippen, described by the sea captain who was responsible for his arrest as 'the acme of politeness'.

As they rose from their banquet to return to headquarters, the ants blundered away from table, limped, staggered, fell to their knees. Their legs kept on waving feebly long after their thoraxes had hit the deck. Quietly cheered by the slaughter, I poured myself a finger of Scotch and went out to sit in my rocker on the porch and admire the scenery.

B eyond the dogwood tree, a rickety flight of steps led down to my own pier and boat-house on this narrow neck of lake. The water, luminously brown after the rain, was pock-marked with the circles of rising fish, and the far shore, a hundred yards or so away, was colonized by a string of ample, single-storey wood-frame houses, each on its acre of green woodland, each with its private dock and electrical boat-hoist. My ant-ridden cabin was by far the poorest house in sight. The standard bungalow in this cosy waterside suburb boasted white Doric pillars in moulded fibreglass, floodlights on the lawn, a barbecue pit big enough to roast a whole bullock and a satellite-dish big enough to detect signs of life on distant planets. Beyond the houses, a slow freight train was stalking through the trees. The intervening water magnified the sound of its whistle—that long low oboe-chord of the American railroad, a sound perfectly contrived to strike a note at once imperious and deeply wounded.

Whisky in hand, I walked down to my boat-house. As my foot touched the pier, it triggered off a series of belly-flop splashes, making me spill my drink. A fallen beech tree, its bark stripped bare, lay out along the water, and turtles were tumbling in from their perches on its trunk. They came in all sizes, from babies the size of silver dollars to grown-ups as big as soup-tureens. They crashed into the lake like a row of falling bricks. I was glad they were shy: a snapping turtle could amputate a whole hand of fingers with a bite, or take a clean half moon of flesh from your calf, if you were caught at close quarters with it.

My forehead snagged a cobweb, slung between the boat-house and the corrugated iron canopy over the pier. As I flinched away, my glass followed the turtles into the lake.

It was how Europeans had always seen American nature—as shockingly bigger, more colourful, more deadly, more exotic, than anything they'd seen at home. When the urban European thought of the countryside, he imagined a version that was hedged, ditched, planted, well-patrolled. The dangerous wildlife—the bears and the wolves—had been exterminated; the few remaining 'wild' animals, like foxes, hares, boars, were permitted to exist only because they provided sport for man. The European landscape was a mixture of park, farm and garden; the nearest it came to wilderness was the keepered grouse moor and the occasional picturesque crag. Europeans were astonished by America, by its irrepressible profusion and 'savagery'.

Hector St John de Crèvecoeur's *Letters from an American*

Farmer, published in 1782, set a tone that has survived for more than two hundred years. America was a place where, if you went on a quiet country stroll, you might come across:

> ... something resembling a cage, suspended to the limbs of a tree, all the branches of which appeared covered with large birds of prey, fluttering about and anxiously endeavouring to perch on the cage. Actuated by an involuntary motion of my hands more than by any design of my mind, I fired at them; they all flew to a short distance, with a most hideous noise, when, horrid to think and painful to repeat, I perceived a Negro, suspended in the cage and left there to expire! I shudder when I recollect that the birds had already picked out his eyes; his cheek-bones were bare; his arms had been attacked in several places; and his body seemed covered with a multitude of wounds. From the edges of the hollow sockets and from the lacerations with which he was disfigured, the blood slowly dropped and tinged the ground beneath. No sooner were the birds flown than swarms of insects covered the whole body of this unfortunate wretch, eager to feed on his mangled flesh and to drink his blood. I found myself suddenly arrested by the power of affright and terror; my nerves were convulsed; I trembled; I stood motionless, involuntarily contemplating the fate of this Negro in all its dismal latitude.

This was de Crèvecoeur's quintessential American scene, and the image of the sightless Negro in the cage, found while botanising in 'a pleasant wood', hangs over the whole of his book like a great question-mark. How could this come to happen? Did exposure to the awful wildness of American nature bring out an answering echo of brute savagery in human nature?

De Crèvecoeur was fascinated by the brilliancy of the humming-bird and by its rapacious temper:

> From what motives I know not, it will tear and lacerate flowers into a hundred pieces, for, strange to tell, they are the most irascible of the feathered tribe. Where do

passions find room in so diminutive a body? They often
fight with the fury of lions until one of the combatants
falls a sacrifice and dies.

Writing about American snakes, he described how the spirit of the
copperhead possessed the body of its human victim:

I have heard only of one person who was stung by a
copperhead in this country. The poor wretch instantly
swelled in a most dreadful manner; a multitude of spots
of different hues alternately appeared and vanished on
different parts of his body; his eyes were filled with
madness and rage; he cast them on all present with the
most vindictive looks; he thrust out his tongue as the
snakes do; he hissed through his teeth with
inconceivable strength and became an object of terror to
all bystanders.

In all these passages there is an undercurrent of suggestion that
Americans have been somehow snakebitten by their natural
surroundings—that something venomous and predatory has
entered the American character. If you live in such proximity to the
alligator, the snake, the vulture and the humming-bird, you will find
that to crucify a Negro in a cage soon comes quite naturally.

For all its seeming facunality, *Letters from an American Farmer*
was a work of fiction. De Crèvecoeur made his America up as he
went along; the book works by symbolic logic, and the truth it tells is
a symbolic truth. However much he stretched the facts of his
country walks and fantasized his natural history, he was true to a
European perception of the United States that has barely altered
since his death.

Two centuries after de Crèvecoeur, a notably cool British
historian, Hugh Brogan, described the battles over civil rights in the
South in the sixties in *The Pelican History of the United States of
America*. He wrote: 'The savagery lurking in American life was
welling to the surface. . . '

I have tried that phrase out, substituting other words for
'American'—and it doesn't work. *The savagery lurking in German
life*? That would betray the writer's Germanophobia. *The savagery
lurking in English life* would have too florid a ring to it. Yet Brogan,

whose understanding and affection for America is matched by no other contemporary European historian's, can allow the phrase to pop out as if it were an accomplished fact. Oh, yes, that lurking kind of *American* savagery ... it is as unexceptionable—as platitudinous—as associating America with the hamburger and Coca Cola.

Back in the rocker I could see a vulture quartering the sky, the snapping turtles on the dead tree, a very large poisoned ant like a collapsing Degas dancer. I had been warned that water-moccasins swam in my dock. I was landlord to a number of invisible brown recluses and probably fire ants as well. I had heard a serpentine slithering in the fallen leaves beyond the bedroom window and could reckon on meeting the odd rattlesnake, copperhead and diamondback. Polecat Hollow was mildly infested with poison oak and poison ivy. Black widow spiders were common. One of the realtors had said that both black bears and cougars were occasionally spotted in the suburbs of Guntersville. There was more savagery lurking in my plot—in the water, up the trees, under the dead leaves, in the woodwork, behind the shower-curtain—than there was in the whole of Europe put together; I had lit on the cradle of American savagery, in the state that harboured more venomous creatures than any other in the Union.

It was a relief to see the lights coming on all round the lake and hear the neighbourly susurration of tyres on distant gravel. There was the smell of barbecue charcoal in the air; evening voices in the trees; the *tink* of ice-cubes in a cocktail glass; someone calling, 'Hon? Hey, hon?'. I swept the bathroom carpet with a straw broom, blackening the dustpan with ant-corpses. Then, too tired to make the journey back to town and seek out strangers for company, I tried to pretend that I really lived here; grilling a sirloin steak, watching *Larry King Live* on television, doing my best to push to the back of my mind the image of the coiled snake and the spider no bigger than the pharmacist's thumb-nail. A discussion of the Minimum Wage went suddenly out of focus and out of earshot, drowned by the sound of something, or somebody, moving in the leaves outside—but it was only a stray breeze eddying from the lake. Across the water, a dog set up an angry yodel and was answered by a bass growl on my side; in a moment, every German shepherd, Dobermann and Rottweiler in the neighbourhood had joined the dog-telegraph. It occurred to me that I must be the only resident of Polecat Hollow who didn't have a dog to warn them of intruders.

I woke at two a.m., to the telephone ringing. There was slow breathing on the line, then the caller hung up. Twenty minutes later, the phone rang again. This time there was a voice. 'Will you quit shittin' me?'

'Look,' I said, 'I'm not—' but he'd gone.

At three a.m. he was back. 'I know you're there, Bri. What you scared of? Afraid of talking, Bri?'

I shouted into the phone that I wasn't Bri, that I was English, that I'd just moved in; but all I got in reply was the dialling tone.

My persecutor left me alone until just before eight, when he, or rather his just-audible breath, was back on the line. I filled the silence with indignant gabble; he cut me short with a click, then the one-note tune of the empty telephone.

I called the real-estate agents, the telephone company and the police department. I was told that the cabin wasn't on a party line—that it had been vacant for several months—that no one called Bri or Brian or Bryant was known to the owners of the place. The woman in the police department said that they'd be happy to help, but only when the voice had made some specific threat, 'like if he says he's going to kill you.'

Who the hell was Bri and what was I doing in his life? If he was usually available for conversation at two and three in the morning, Bri kept foxy hours. I had found a half-eaten plate of tortilla chips on the breakfast bar: were they his? Had he been squatting here secretly for weeks and moved out only when he saw me moving in? What had he done to provoke the spook, and why should the spook be so unsurprised to hear Bri putting on a phoney British accent and pretending to be someone else?

Sleep-starved and jumpy, I raced ahead on Bri's biography. He'd ratted on a drugs deal—maybe run off with the stash. The cabin in Polecat Hollow had afforded him a quiet asylum until I'd shown up; and now his friend, having tracked him down to a phone number, would soon be round to finish off whatever business was still outstanding . . . Did this taciturn friend actually know what Bri looked like? If the friendship was based on the trade in crack, coke or heroin, friends had very often never met their friends.

Quit shittin' me, Bri—.

I stood by the gas cooker, glumly watching for signs of life in the glass belvedere on the domed top of the percolator. A trickle of water popped into view and disappeared. Where was Bri now? I saw him Huck Finning it out in the woods, lying low, waiting to see what my next move would be.

The phone rang again. '*Bri?*' This time it was a woman, and this time she heard me out. 'Must've got a wrong number,' she said; but then she called again.

'Who *is* this?'

'What number are you dialling?'

'Five eight two, three two seven three,' she said, stretching the vowels out like so many lengths of knicker-elastic.

'That's *my* number. That's not Bri's. I've never heard of Bri—'

'That's the number Bri goes under. Five eight two . . . aw, shit,' and she hung up on me.

I knew Bri, or at least Bri's kind. He'd be twenty-three or -four, with skinny whippet bones; thin fair hair, spread over his low forehead like stalks of mouldy hay; no lips, chips of dull flint for eyes, cheek-bones like axe-blades. Bri was the kind of person who gets killed in back alleys outside bars.

This was absurd. I was winding myself up with old Travis McGee stories. I sat out on the porch with a mug of coffee and studied the dogwood blossom, the ruffled water, the Spirit parked sedately on the driveway. I identified the white flashes on the wings of a passing mocking-bird. I was sitting in the middle of a life so sunlit, so comfortably suburban, that nothing could be badly wrong in it.

The phone was mewling in its cradle again. I let it go on crying. I thought, all I need is a German shepherd to keep watch at night; a dog with a basso-profundo voice to scare my spook back into the woods and out of my dreams.

The man in God's Kritturs was tending a bank of illuminated aquariums. 'You want to . . . borrow . . . a dog. For a . . . month.' He straightened up and turned round to face me.

'Well, I thought more like—rent.'

'Rent *a* Dawg.'

'I've got a spook-caller, in the small hours—'

He smiled patiently. In the pet shop business, you get to meet all kinds of crazy people. ''Fraid I just can't help you there,' he said, 'but if a Siamese fighting fish was any good to you . . . '

William the pharmacist suggested the dog pound at the Animal Hospital on Henry Street, where I raised only a faint zephyr of amusement ('Gentleman here wants a tempo-rary, re-turn-able dog') and was shown to the cells at the back of the building. The dogs were short of ears, eyes, fur and teeth. They had the resigned manners of long-term detainees. Some slept, whiffling asthmatically; some raised a single bored eye as I peered at them through the wire. One growled, but it was a counter-tenor, not a bass, and I could see Bri's friend skying it contemptuously—a brindled football, sailing over the lake, hitting top C as it went. It wouldn't do.

A technician came over to say: 'You looking to borrow a dog? I got a dog you can borrow if you want.' She occupied every available inch of an outsize T-shirt that asked *Have You Hugged Your Horse Today?* 'She's a black lab, she's *trained*. She's old, but she still barks real good at strangers in the night.'

'And she won't mind?'

'Gypsy? No, she'll just mooch all the love out of you she can. She's a big love-dog.'

'Won't you miss her?'

'I got more dogs out at my place'n I can keep a count of. You want to borrow my dog, you're most welcome.'

So at noon I followed Janet Potocki out to her place 'on the mountain'; a ten-mile drive that led from highway to crooked lane to dirt road to rutted track. The isolated farms still looked like bold and novel intrusions on the forest, even though their white shingles were flaked and scabby and some were drifting from decrepitude into ruin. Bony cattle stood up to their knees in the swollen creeks. Old men in dungarees stopped in their work to check out what a Spirit with New York plates was doing hereabouts, and farm dogs shifted grudgingly from their sleeping-quarters in the middle of the road to let our cars go by.

The Potocki place was a trailer on several acres of its own green hilltop. Mountains were cheap in Alabama. Here even someone working for something close to the minimum wage of 3.35 dollars an hour could be the landed proprietor of a handsome estate. Away from the town and the main highway, this kind of mixed woodland and rough pasture went for around 400 dollars an acre. I'd seen tracts of it, in thirty- and forty-acre lots, advertised in the Classified section of the *Gleam*. For sixty dollars down and sixty dollars a month, you could buy a fine parcel of American wilderness on which to improvise an *ad hoc*, self-reliant life. A second-hand trailer home could be had for less than 3,000 dollars . . . The man who sold bird whistles in Manhattan might have set up as a country squire in Marshall County, Alabama.

As we pulled up, a horse shoved its head into the open window of my car. I nervously patted the bridge of its nose, feeling incompetently urban and out of touch with these rural courtesies. A troupe of dogs clowned and tumbled round Ms Potocki, breaking off every few seconds to yell at me to go home where I came from. 'Gypsy? Gypsy!' Then, to me, 'There's your dog—'

She was by far the staidest of the troupe; plump and matronly, with big teats and a grizzled face. She waddled as she walked towards me, a little stiff with rheumatism in her hindquarters. The skin of her forehead was wrinkled in a puzzled frown. Her tail swayed uncertainly from side to side. She had shy caramel eyes. The words 'black lab' had conveyed to me something altogether more fierce and coyote-like than this faded old biddy, who was deferentially sniffing at my shoes.

I could see Gypsy cowering under the bed if the spook ever phoned again, let alone showed up in person. 'She can bark?'

'If I wasn't here with you, Gypsy'd see you right off the property. That's a trained dog. You just give her a bit of love and see she gets fed right, she'll be real good protection for you.'

With Gypsy following behind, tail at half-mast, we went into the trailer. It was hot, cramped, overpoweringly doggy. A spaniel with a litter of week-old pups lay in a basket at the foot of the narrow bed. The floor was carpeted with newspapers on which the dog-troupe had strewn bits of food. For the dogs' entertainment, *As the World Turns* was playing on the TV. The horse pressed its long head against the trailer window and neighed to be let in.

Looking out over the valley to the vaporous blue of the next range of hills, I said: 'You've got a wonderful view. It's great out here.'

'Well, it suits me.'

Certainly her life in the trailer on the hillside looked as chosen, as wanted, as Thoreau's in his log cabin in the woods. By suburban standards it was bare and makeshift; it did smell strongly of dog-farts; but there was no hint of quiet desperation in it. If I imagined someone like Janet Potocki in England, I saw her as thwarted and unhappy. There, it would be painfully hard to be in your mid-twenties, too large for society, too poor and constrained to make an independent break. But here she was free; working happily, part-time, in the Animal Hospital, comfortably supporting herself, her acres, her family of animals out on the mountain. I doubted if anyone thought of her as cracked or eccentric to live like this. The mountains were made for nonconformists, and there was still a soft spot in American culture for the idea of going it alone on your own private frontier.

'My parents didn't like me living out here by myself; not at first. They got used to it. I told them I was a whole lot safer up here with the dogs than they are down in the city . . . '

Gypsy had fallen instantly asleep on Janet Potocki's bed, looking more like a stranded dugong than a dog; my blind date. It was too late to stand her up now, with Ms Potocki fetching her collar and lead, her tin feeding-bowl, her rations of Canine Maintenance—brown vegetable pellets that looked like the artificial soil in which people keep rubber plants in pots. At the sound of the dry rattle of food in the paper sack, the dog opened an eye and crooned. A trickle of frothy saliva leaked on to the bedspread.

'She may like to eat some candy on the drive.' Doing my best to hide my feelings, I pocketed half a dozen bright red miniature bones. 'She *loves* candy, don't you, honey?'

The dog raised herself carefully, in sections, clambered off the bed and took a candy-bone. She ate messily, with her mouth open, showing her tartarous back teeth.

She frowned gravely at the Spirit but after some havering she consented to park her considerable butt on the passenger seat. As we drove away, I bribed her with candy-bones, dolefully accepted.

'Gypsy . . . hey, Gypsy? Gypsy?'

Silence. She stared back at me, her eyes full of guarded incomprehension, as if I'd asked her what she thought of

Deconstructionism or SDI. It was one of those dates. Her tongue sneaked out sideways and licked a crumb of candy out of her grey whiskers.

As we passed a farm dog in the road, Gypsy suddenly gave voice. It was a fine growl, that started with a low bubbling deep in the bronchii and developed into a sound like a car engine from which the muffler has fallen off. I was thrilled.

'Good dog! That's a *good* dog!' I put my arm round her neck and stroked her shoulder. She tilted her nose to the roof and sniffed sadly.

Back on the highway, we overtook a car with another Labrador sitting up in the back seat. As we drew level, Gypsy planted her forepaws on the dashboard and ululated like a dinner gong. It was music in my ears. I fed her a candy-bone with the solicitude of a newly infatuated lover.

The telephone was ringing when we reached the cabin. Gypsy, nose to the ground, padded off on a tour of inspection. I picked up the receiver.

'Bri, you mad at me or something?' A woman's voice.

'I'm not Bri—' The phone clattered to the floor out of my hand; Gypsy had found an interesting tid-bit in the corner of the room—a poisoned ant trap on a square of card. I threw myself at the dog and wrestled her away from the glob of clear syrup to which she had already begun to extend her long, pleasure-seeking tongue. It was like trying to shift a Welsh dresser. There was a great deal more black Labrador than met the eye. Her frown darkened. For a moment, she tolerated my pushing and shoving as a boisterous game. Then she drew her lips back round her teeth and snarled.

'Gypsy—Oh, Gypsy. I'm sorry, Gypsy. Sorry, dog.'

I produced the last of the candy-bones from my pocket and handed it to her on my open palm. She disdained to take it and sat, quite silent now, with an expression of fierce wounded dignity in her eyes. When I moved my hand closer, there was a warning growl deep in her throat.

She watched me as I gathered up the ant traps. I flushed them down the w.c. and washed my hands. When I came back into the living-room, Gypsy was standing beside the door, tail tucked tightly between her legs, motioning at the door-handle with her nose.

'I'm sorry, Gypsy. You don't understand. Please, dog?'

I filled her bowl with Canine Maintenance and rattled it enticingly at her. She didn't move. I presented her with a soup-plate of water. I laid the red candy-bone at her feet.

'Please? Come on, Gypsy.'

But she had eyes only for the door. She gave me to understand that the only way in which she wished to communicate with me in future was through her lawyer. I thought, I have been here before. I got down on my knees and talked to her, saying that I was sorry, that it was all a big misunderstanding, that I'd make it up to her in any way I could. She stared me down. I hadn't known that dogs were capable of looking so implacably righteous, so *I've done everything in my power* and *it's not* my *selfishness we're talking about here.*

The moment required some dramatic concession on my part. I held out no great hopes for the strategy, but I got out the remaining three-quarter-pound tranche of rib-eye steak from the fridge and unwrapped it from its cellophane-and-cardboard tray.

'Gypsy?'

She frowned, stared, slowly unglued herself from her position at the door. I cut an inch-square cube from the steak and held it out to her. She took it, chewed and was transformed. She began to prance. Her tail was drumming on the door of the Frigidaire as she flung herself from side to side, tongue lolling, hindquarters executing a series of froglike vertical jumps. Throwing rheumatism and injured womanhood to the winds, Gypsy reverted to puppydom. I cut up the rest of the meat and carried it in scooped handfuls to her bowl, where she vacuumed up every last scrap in less than a minute. The moment she was through, she came back to the Frigidaire, laid her jaw on the carpet between her forepaws, rolled her eyes back and moaned devoutly at the closed door.

'No more.' I showed her empty hands. She studied the gesture cross-eyedly and moaned some more. The scything motion of her tail gradually slowed, and she rose, a little stiffly, to lick the hands that were still bloody from the holy meat.

We drove back to town, to Food Land ('Home Folks Serving Home Folks'), where I bought five pounds of chuck steak. It came to about the same price as a bouquet of roses. Back at Polecat Hollow, Gypsy shouldered her way ahead of me into the cabin and stationed herself at the door of the Frigidaire as if we'd been doing this for years.

At sunset, when the dog-telegraph began, Gypsy stood out on the porch and bayed on cue; a gruesome eldritch tremolo that echoed through the woods and over the darkening water. She was doing me proud. I scribbled a marginal note on the page of a book I was reading for review, feeling as snugly domestic as any householder in the hollow.

Both the dog and I needed exercising. On the levee next morning, Gypsy, fuelled by a large steak breakfast, went lolloping ahead; nose down, ears out sideways, her creaky hindquarters a little out of sync with her plunging front end. Her record as a guard dog so far was patchy. She had slept through two spook calls during the evening, but an hour ago she'd summoned me from the house with an urgent, gravelly snarling. I had braced myself for an encounter with one of Bri's business associates and found Gypsy bravely standing her ground against a floppy yellow butterfly in the dogwood tree.

Even though I'd disconnected the phone at midnight, I had had little sleep. To begin with, the dog had curled herself up meekly on the floor at the foot of the bed, but at one a.m. I woke half-suffocated by a ton of dog sprawled full-length against me on the coverlet. Afraid of another scene of mute recrimination and suitcase-packing, I let her stay. She was not a considerate bedfellow. She snored; she hogged the bed; she dribbled copiously. Twice she thrust her muzzle into my face, and not gently, because she wanted to go and pee in the yard. When at five a.m. I switched on the bedside light and tried to read, I saw us both reflected in the mirror tiles on the ceiling: a large black dog in a state of luxurious abandon; a haggard man with bags under his eyes, living, like the dog's household pet, in a state of resigned subjection.

FREE THINKING.

First Three Issues Free. Take out a trial subscription to the London Review of Books and see what you think about Britain's boldest literary journal.

Perhaps it's because our contributors are among the best writers – and boldest thinkers – of the day.

Or perhaps it's because we encourage these writers to take sides on important issues... welcoming their wit even when we disagree with their wisdom.

Whatever the reason, the London Review of Books has become Britain's boldest literary journal. And one thing is certain – if you haven't seen a recent copy, you've missed a very stimulating read. About subjects as varied as 'Games, Sex and Evolution'... 'Fascism and the Mafia'...'The History of the Potato'...'The Psychology of Personal Identity' ...'Constructive Drinking'..and 'Wittgenstein.'

You've also missed great writing by Craig Raine, Angela Carter, James Fenton, Frank Kermode, Alan Bennett, Marina Warner, Julian Barnes and Andrew Boyle, to name just a few of the recent contributors to the London Review of Books.

However, there's no need to miss any more. Take this opportunity to request a trial subscription, and receive three issues free. If after receiving your free issues, you are less than satisfied, you may cancel your subscription and receive a full refund.

ſinstitut français

In the heart of South Kensington the French Institute offers an ideal venue for a wide range of cultural events: seminars, conferences, exhibitions, theatre, dance and film seasons.

Its facilities include the largest reference and lending French language library in the U.K. (75,000 volumes).

The French Institute is equally the official centre for French language teaching and offers a large selection of high quality courses (general – secretarial – business – academic) given by native French teachers.

COLLOQUE, CONFERENCE, CONVEGNO, COLOQUIO, CONFERENCIA, KONFERENZ
"What form could the narrative discourse take today"
9, 10, 11 FEBRUARY 1990

Why?

By the end of the fifties the Nouveau Roman attempted to answer the question posed by modernism:

'What form could the narrative discourse take today?'

It seemed that Balzac had become the 'aunt Sally' of a whole generation of critics and theorists.

Thirty years have elapsed, MODERNISM has, as we are told, given birth to POST-MODERNISM. What is today in France understood by LITERARY CREATIVITY and PARTICULARLY IN THE NOVEL?

How?

Five young novelists will propose their answers to this question:–

- Marianne ALPHANT, novelist, literary correspondent at Libération. She collaborated with the American choreographer Susan Buirge by writing 'supporting texts'.
- Patrick DEVILLE. Born in France and lived for a number of years in Africa and The Middle East. Author of 'Cordon Bleu' and 'Longue-vue'.
- Jean ECHENOZ author of 'Cherokee' (Seuil, 1983, Prix Médicis 1983) and other works.
- Olivier ROLIN, whose latest work 'Sept villes' has been published by Rivages, 1988.
- Jean-Philippe TOUSSAINT, author of 'La Salle de Bain', 'Monsieur', 'L'Appareil Photo', (Editions de Minuit 1985, 1986 & 1989).

In France, in Europe:

The French Institute, in collaboration with the representatives of other European Cultural Centres in London, seeks to broaden the debate: authors and literary critics from Britain, France, Germany, Italy, Portugal and Spain will form a round table for a state of the art discussion remembering as Levi-Strauss says: 'Aware of it or not, one never advances alone on the path of creativity.' Particularly in this new 'fin de siècle'.

Events around the Conference:

A destructuration of different genres which encourages fluidity and the passage from one artistic form to another is illustrated by:

- 'La Salle de Bain': a film based on a novel by Jean-Philippe TOUSSAINT (British Premiere)
- Photographic Exhibition by Butor and Plossu and paintings Pratsevall and Butor
- 'Exercices de Style': a stage performance by Jaques SEILER, based on Queneau (British Premiere).

In collaboration with: The Independent, Le Magazine Littéraire, Gallimard, Seuil, P.O.L. . . . .

For further details on membership and the conference telephone or write to:

INSTITUT FRANÇAIS DE LONDRES
17 QUEENSBERRY PLACE, LONDON SW7
Telephone 01 589 6211

Nicholson Baker
ROOM TEMPERATURE

What are the questions that occur to Mike,
our narrator, part-time technical writer
and reviewer of television advertisements,
as he feeds a bottle of warmed evaporated
milk to his six-month old baby daughter
Bug at three-fifteen on an autumn afternoon?

These are some of them:

At what speed does a puff of air travel across a still room
(on an autumn day, at approximately three-fifteen in the
afternoon) when the windows are closed?

When (and why) does the act of smiling sound like bacon frying?

Under exactly what circumstances can married partners
become too intimate?

Room Temperature, is Nicholson Baker's second novel. His first,
The Mezzanine, taking place before, during and after the lunch
hour, is an original kind of fiction: the novel of the office.

In **Room Temperature**, taking place before, during and after
another kind of lunch hour, (the bottle-feeding of Bug), Nicholson
Baker gives us another kind of fiction: the novel of the home.

The Mezzanine is a seriously funny book.
Things (shoe-laces, drinking straws,
ear-plugs) will never seem the same again.'
Salman Rushdie.

ISBN: 0 140 14212 6

April publication, hardback £11.99.
Simultaneous publication, in paperback,
of The Mezzanine. £4.99

ISBN: 0 140 14002 6

Notes on Contributors

Graham Swift is the author of four novels and one collection of short stories. **Neal Ascherson** has been reporting on Eastern Europe for' over thirty years and has recently joined *The Independent on Sunday*. **Michael Ignatieff**, the author of *A Just Measure of Pain, The Needs of Strangers* and *The Russian Album*, has completed a novel set in the Soviet Union that will be published later this year. **Patrick Zachmann** applied eight times for a visa to take photographs in Georgia before he was finally admitted. His photographs of Hong Kong appeared in *Granta 29*. **Victoria Tokareva** lives in Moscow and has completed a collection of stories. **Ludmilla Petrushevskaya** is a short-story writer and playwright. A longer version of 'Our Circle' is published in Petrushevskaya's first collection of stories, still not published in English, entitled *Immortal Love*. Tokareva and Petrushevskaya, along with Tatyana Tolstaya, are regarded as being in the vanguard of a new generation of Soviet fiction writers. **Josef Škvorecký** left Czechoslovakia after the Russian invasion of Prague in 1968 and settled in Canada, where he is a lecturer at the University of Toronto and where, concurrently, he is running the émigré publishing house, '68. His most recent book is *Talkin' Moscow Blues*. **George Steiner's** 'Noël, Noël' was in *Granta* 28. *Real Presences* was published last spring. **Jurek Becker** is one of East Germany's best known authors. He was born in Lódź in 1937 and spent his early childhood in the Jewish ghetto and concentration camps. The poet **Hans Magnus Enzensberger** lives in Munich. His most recent book is *Europe, Europe*. **Werner Krätschell** was born in Berlin. He is a Dean in the German Protestant Church, overseeing twenty-four parishes in the Pankow district of Berlin, and has been a leading figure of the opposition. **Isaiah Berlin** is a Fellow of All Souls College, Oxford, and has written widely on Russian thinkers in the nineteenth century. **Andrei Sinyavsky** was born in Moscow in 1925. His pseudonymously published essay, 'What is Social Realism?' led to his arrest and his being sentenced to seven years in a labour camp. Since 1973 he has lived in Paris, where he edits the émigré literary magazine, *Syntaxis*. In his piece

Sinyavsky mentions the dismissal last November of the editor of *October*; the editor is Anatoly Ananyer and the anti-Soviet work published in the magazine was an extract from Sinyavsky's own book on Pushkin. **Abraham Brumberg** is a contributor to and editor of *Chronicle of a Revolution: A Western-Soviet Inquiry* to be published shortly. **Noel Annan** supervised the development of German political parties in the British Zone of occupied Germany after the War. The poet **Günter Kunert** joined the Social Democratic Party in 1949 but was expelled in 1976 for protesting the expatriation of Wolf Biermann. He now lives in West Germany on an East German visa. **Tony Benn** is the Labour Member of Parliament for Chesterfield and the author of *Arguments for Socialism*. Czesław Miłosz is the author of *The Captive Mind*. In 1980 he was awarded the Nobel Prize for Literature. Last summer he was able to return to Poland. **Ivan Klíma** was banned from publishing in the aftermath of the 1968 Soviet invasion of Czechoslovakia. His books, until now all published abroad, include *My First Loves* and *A Summer Affair*. *Love and Garbage* will be published in Britain in the spring. **Mircea Dinescu** has been under house-arrest since 22 April 1989 and is watched over by eighteen police officials. The poet and critic **Stephen Spender** was a founding editor of *Encounter*. **Yuri Ribchinsky** was born in the Ukraine in 1935. He is currently embarked on a project of photographing Soviet village life. **Mikhail Steblin-Kamensky's** account of the Siege of Leningrad was written during the war but was not published until 1989. **Vladimir Filonov** is one of the Soviet Union's most accomplished photographers, who, at the age of forty-one, has taken part in 280 exhibitions and received 128 awards. 'Dying Village' is a part of a series on Russia's roads. The poet **Joseph Brodsky** was born in Leningrad in 1940. After being exiled as a dissident and 'social parasite', he emigrated to the United States in 1972. His books include *A Part of Speech* and *Less Than One*, a collection of essays, published in 1986. He was awarded the Nobel Prize for Literature in 1987. The first part of **Jonathan Raban**'s 'New World' appeared in *Granta* 29. Raban was sighted, shortly before this issue went to press, somewhere in the state of Washington.